THE CROSS

Hans-Ruedi Weber

THE CROSS

Tradition and Interpretation

Translated by Elke Jessett

William B. Eerdmans Publishing Company
Grand Rapids, Michigan 49503

First published in German as *Kreuz:*
Überlieferung und Deutung der Kreuzigung
Jesu im Neutestamentlichen Kulturraum
by Kreuz Verlag, Stuttgart and Berlin

© Kreuz Verlag Stuttgart 1975

First published in English 1979, by SPCK, London.
This American edition published 1979 by special arrangement with SPCK

Translation © The Society for Promoting Christian Knowledge 1978

Library of Congress Cataloging in Publication Data

Weber, Hans Ruedi.
  The cross.

  Translation of Kreuz.
  Bibliography: p. 140.
  1. Jesus Christ—Crucifixion. I. Title.
BT450.W413   232.9'63   78-17529
ISBN 0-8028-1739-4

Printed in Great Britain

Contents

CONTENTS

Note

This present book represents the first four chapters of a study which was published, with extensive footnotes, under the title: *Kreuz und Kultur: Deutungen der Kreuzigung Jesu in neutestamentlichen Kulturen der Gegenwart* (Geneva 1975). The chapters not included here covered:

5: The Hazards of Translation: results of an inquiry among Bible translators regarding the difficulties of translating the message of the crucifixion.
6: Artists as Interpreters of the Crucifixion: summary of the lines of development of artistic interpretation of the crucifixion through the ages and in present-day cultures.
7: A Message for Today: summary and critical survey of the results of case studies in America, Asia, Africa, Europe, and the Middle East about the way in which the message of the crucifixion is understood, preached, and lived by church members.

Copies of the full study (in German) may be obtained from: Department for Bible Studies, World Council of Churches, 150 route de Ferney, Ch 1211, Geneva 20, Switzerland.

Introduction

'If we are to be threatened with death, then we want to die in freedom; let the executioner, the shrouding of the head and the very name of the cross be banished from the body and life of Roman citizens, and from their thoughts, eyes and ears.'

'For Jews demand signs and Greeks seek wisdom, but we preach Christ crucified—a stumbling block to Jews and folly to Gentiles.'

The first quotation comes from Cicero. For him, the great defender of classical culture, crucifixion was the expression of the worst barbarism. He had earlier condemned this 'most cruel and hideous form of execution'. Now, in his defence of the aged Roman senator and banker, C. Rabirius, who stood accused of high treason, Cicero declared in the Roman forum in the year 63 B.C. that even the mere idea of crucifixion ought to be banned.

The crucifixion of a man is indeed irreconcilable with humanism of whatever hue. Every crucifixion casts doubt on man's claim to civilization. Civilization, after all, means that ordering of nature and of human co-existence which allows individuals to develop fully with their fellow humans and within their environment. When a man, no matter who, is tortured and put to death in as cruel a manner as by crucifixion, it must lead to a crisis of human civilization.

Why was it then that in public places of the Roman Empire about a hundred years after Cicero, another thinker of the classical world, the Apostle Paul, proclaimed the crucifixion of a man as the essence of his message of joy? Why is it that in the past nineteen centuries in Christian churches the world over the remembrance of this crucifixion has been at the very heart of divine services?

The Paradox of the Cross

We are confronted here by the paradox between Christian
faith and human civilization. What seemed to be the
ignominious end to Christ's story has become the victory of
God's cause. The crisis of man's aspirations to civilization
became at the same time the centre of all human civilization.
Those who, like Cicero, avert their eyes, ears, and thoughts
from the fact that the capacity to crucify is deeply rooted in
the individual and in human society, do not base their claims
to civilization on the realities of our world and our times. If a
man, for the sake of justice and love, deliberately chose the
way to the cross and while on that cross—the pinnacle of
human cruelty—was able still to be just and loving, then
through him human aspirations to civilization are given
promise.

In the history of mankind this paradoxical truth has time
and again been divined. The myths of gods and heroes who
died and returned to earth must, however, be interpreted as
having their origins in the celebration of the cycle of nature
rather than as an expression of this paradoxical truth. It is
different with Plato who, in his discussion of justice, has
Glaucon describing a truly just man. He sees him as 'a man of
true simplicity of character who . . . wants to *be* and not to
seem good. We must indeed not allow him to seem good, for
if he does he will have all the rewards and honours paid to the
man who has a reputation for justice, and we should not be
able to tell whether his motive is love of justice or love of the
rewards and honours. No, we must strip him of everything
except his justice . . . he must have the worst of reputations
for wrong-doing even though he has done no wrong, so we
can test his justice and see if he weakens in the face of
unpopularity and all that goes with it. We shall give him an
undeserved and lifelong reputation for wickedness and make
him stick to his chosen course until his death. . . . They will
say that the just man, as we have pictured him, will be
scourged, tortured, and imprisoned, his eyes will be put out
and after enduring every humiliation he will be crucified . . .'
(*Republic*. Penguin, 2nd rev. edn, pp. 107–8). Small wonder
that Plato's astonishing description of a truly just man was

soon taken by the early Church as a prophecy of Christ.

But it is not only the occidental world that provides the occasional glimpses of the mystery of the cross. Most cultures have developed sacrificial rites. Whatever the nature of the sacrifice and however it may be explained, both individuals and societies have somehow sensed that the reality of human nature and of the world we live in does not provide a direct path towards all-embracing peace, full humanity, and civilization. Time and again human greed, vainglory, and fear have led to fratricide, war, and crucifixion. Only a sacrifice can break this satanic circle. Neither societies nor individuals can find true identity through self-assertion; only by transcending self, by devotion to a cause which leads far beyond present existence can this be achieved.

The Course of the Present Study

It might be illuminating to undertake a historical study—from the point of view of religious and cultural history—of these premonitions and gropings of different civilizations towards the mystery of the cross. The concern of this present study, however, is exclusively the event of the crucifixion which probably took place outside Jerusalem on 7 April, in A.D. 30. Our concern here is not with the fate of any righteous man or with sacrifice in general, but with the death of Jesus of Nazareth, a Jew, who was condemned by the Roman prefect Pontius Pilate.

Chapter 1 summarizes what is known today about the historical event of Christ's crucifixion, based on archaeological discoveries, Roman jurisprudence, medical experiments, biblical and literary sources.

In the following three chapters we shall examine how the first generations of the Church discovered the importance of the crucifixion and how the message of this important event was variously interpreted, celebrated, and preached in those parts of the ancient world where the New Testament took root.

It is, after all, quite astonishing that this repugnant event gained such central importance for the Christian faith. Chapter 2, therefore, is an attempt to trace the earliest Christian interpretations of what happened at Golgotha. Which were the oral and perhaps even written traditions that were developed in the pre-canonic era?

Chapter 3 deals with two texts from St Paul: the one about the cross from 1 Cor. 1.23 already quoted at the beginning of this introduction, and the theology of the cross which Paul formulated in his dispute with the communities of Galatia (Gal. 1.13ff). This is intended to demonstrate that the message of the cross can never be preached in general terms, in a vacuum. It always represents the challenge of a definite situation, where the crucified Christ leads to a crisis of certain human aspirations and where he is at the same time proclaimed as the essence of a new human existence. Although the Christian faith knows no other gospel than that of the crucified and risen Christ, this one gospel can and must nevertheless be differently preached in different situations. This will become clear in Chapter 4, which examines the accounts of the crucifixion given by the four Evangelists. These took the traditions handed down to them regarding the crucifixion extremely seriously, and passed much of it on in their Gospels. With an eye to the different situations of the communities for which they wrote, they did, however, vary the emphases of their accounts.

Christ on the cross can be close to man in many ways. In liturgical drama the encounter may be highly emotional. When we suffer for the sake of righteousness, we can recognize him as the one who has led the way to suffering. If we meditate on the events at Golgotha in the context of twentieth century culture, he can open up new perspectives for us about the meaning of his dying.

In order to examine, though, whether he really is the crucified Christ, the Church must in all periods and all cultures return to the 'passion texts' of the Old Testament, to St Paul's theology of the cross, and to the Evangelists' accounts of the crucifixion (see also Note, p. ix).

It is hoped that the present study will provide some help in retracing the way to the sources, and thence to following our crucified Lord and bearing witness in the context of our present-day culture.

1

The Event of the Crucifixion

1 *The Harsh Reality of Crucifixion*

'I know that the cross will be my grave. This is where my
ancestors, my father, grandfather, and great-grandfather
were buried.' The Roman writer of comedies, Plautus, put
this answer to a threat into the mouth of a slave. One should
of course not take it too literally, but it points to the historical
reality that in Rome crucifixion was essentially a penalty for
slaves. Probably invented by the Persians, crucifixion was
adopted by Alexander the Great and more particularly the
Phoenicians. From the latter it was taken over by the
Romans, who punished not only slaves, but temple robbers
and deserters in this manner. During the slave rebellions they
instituted mass crucifixions.

i *A Slave's Death*

The Greek historian Dionysios Halicarnassensis, a contemporary of Jesus, in what was probably an eyewitness account
of a Roman feast, relates the initial stages of the crucifixion
of a slave. 'A Roman of some note had handed over a slave to
his fellow slaves for them to execute him. In order to make
the punishment generally known, their master ordered them
to drag the condemned man first through the forum and
other public places and to scourge him while doing so. . . .
The slaves who had been thus commanded stretched out both
the man's arms and tied them to a piece of wood which
reached across breast and shoulders to his wrists. They
chased him and lacerated his naked body with their lashes.
Overcome by this cruel treatment, the convict not only
uttered the most heartrending cries, but under the painful
impact of the lashes he also made indecent movements.'

Quite apart from biblical accounts, the further course of

death by crucifixion can be reconstructed fairly clearly from various eyewitness accounts of classical authors, from Roman law, the Talmud, and the accounts of the church Fathers. Sometimes the condemned had a tablet, stating the *causa poena*, the reason for his conviction, hung around his neck. He then had himself to carry the transverse bar of the cross (the *patibulum*) to the place of execution. There he was undressed and scourged, if this had not already been done. According to ancient custom, the executioners were allowed to distribute the condemned man's clothing among themselves. At the place of execution there usually already stood a pole (*stipes* or *palu*) which may also have occasionally served for execution without a transverse bar. The convict was then laid on the ground, both forearms or wrists were tied or nailed to the transverse bar, and he was then raised by the *patibulum*, either up to a groove on the top of the pole (*crux comissa:* T) or up to an indentation on the upper part of the pole (*crux immissa:* +). If the condemned man was intended to be visible from afar, the high cross was chosen. Usually, though, the pole measured no more than about seven feet. This meant that wild animals could tear the crucified man apart. The feet of the victim were not supported by a footrest as Christian art has depicted it since the seventh century, but were tied or nailed to the pole. Usually, the condemned man 'sat' on a peg (*sedile* or *cornu*) which was fixed to the middle of the pole. In one of his letters Seneca quotes the following prayer of Maecenas: 'This (life) preserve for me when I sit on the hard cross.'

This 'sitting on the cross' explains why the crucified languished on it for hours and even days. There exists extensive medical literature about the causes of death by crucifixion, yet this has so far not yielded unanimous conclusions. These studies, as a rule, do not examine crucifixion in general, but Christ's remarkably quick death as recounted in the Gospels. This was probably due to traumatic shock, if indeed one insists on searching for natural causes. Generally, the crucified died of gradual asphyxiation. With increasing exhaustion they were unable to keep upright, even where the cross had a *sedile* and although their feet were tied to the pole. Breathing would become more and more difficult as a result, and this would lead to asphyxiation. This conjecture is supported by the fact that, according to ancient accounts, in order to shorten the agonies of crucifixion, the victim's lower thighs were shattered (*crurifragium*).

It will probably never be possible to give an account of crucifixions and the related causes of death that would be correct in every detail, simply because the manner in which they were carried out varied with the whims of the executioners.

This becomes clear in the description Flavius Josephus gives of mass crucifixions during the siege of Jerusalem in A.D. 70, on the orders of the man who was to become the Roman Emperor Titus: 'Only hunger gave them (i.e. the Jews besieged in Jerusalem) the courage to venture outside the city. . . . If they were caught, however, . . . they were . . . scourged and subjected to all kinds of torture, before being put to death by crucifixion opposite the city walls. Titus was by no means blind to their horrible plight, particularly as every day 500 or more prisoners were brought in. . . . He hoped that this gruesome sight might induce the Jews to surrender, since the same fate awaited them unless they gave themselves up. The soldiers in their rage and hatred had their sport with the prisoners and nailed each one to the cross in a different position. Soon there was no more room for the crosses and no more crosses for the bodies, as there were so many.'

ii The Crucifixion of Rebels in Palestine

Crucifixion as a capital punishment for slaves was well known throughout the ancient world, since it was also used in the provinces of the Roman Empire as a deterrent to rebels. Josephus's text above provides an abundantly clear example.

When the Emperor Augustus in A.D. 9 incorporated Judaea into the Roman Empire, Sulpinius Quirinus, the legate of Syria, was ordered to conduct a census so as to facilitate the collection of taxes. This rekindled the fire of Jewish resistance and led to rebellion under the first prefect of Judaea, Coponius. Josephus gives the following account: 'During his term of office, a man from Galilee, by the name of Judas, incited the inhabitants of the province to secede, declaring it an outrage for them to continue to pay their taxes to Rome and thus recognize any other overlords but God.' Judas, the Galilean, perished and his followers dispersed (cf. Acts 5.37). The rebellion turned into ever-increasing guerilla warfare finally leading to the first Jewish war and to the mass crucifixions. Two sons of Judas were crucified during the period of Tiberius Alexander's Protectorate (A.D. 46–8).

At the beginning of the Jewish war, A.D. 66, Menahem, Judas's third son, seized the fortress of Masada. Imbued with messianic claims, he later attempted to assume the leadership of the rebellion, but was murdered by the followers of another group of Jewish rebels. Thereupon a relation of Judas, Eleazar Ben Yair, retreated with Menahem's surviving followers to the desert fortress of Masada, where they continued their embittered resistance beyond the fall of Jerusalem until their tragic end in A.D. 73.

Judas, the Galilean, and the resistance movement led by him and his family dynasty, is generally referred to in connection with the Zealots' movement. This, however, is open to doubt. It is probable that there were several movements, frequently at loggerheads among themselves, and that Judas's movement—the Sikarians—were initially dominant, while the Zealots only organized themselves into a coherent force during Menahem's time, in A.D. 66–7. It is therefore erroneous to maintain that Jesus died between two Zealots. It is likely, though, that he was crucified between two religio-political rebels.

There is a tendency today to overstress this 'political incarnation' of Jesus, just as formerly too little was made of it. It is improbable that there existed a national, centrally organized army of guerillas before the Jewish war, and in Jesus's day there were probably no more than a few thousand Sikarians. Yet in a small occupied country like Palestine, even a few fanatical groups could cause a great deal of unrest. Religio-political unrest, violent rebellion, and its even more violent repression were characteristic elements of the everyday life of Jesus, his contemporaries, and his disciples. The crucifixion of Jesus must be seen in this religio-political context and cannot be considered in isolation from it.

In the Palestine of that period, crucifixion of rebels was

nothing out of the ordinary. According to Josephus's probably exaggerated account, 2,000 Jewish rebels were crucified
on the mountains around Jerusalem at about the time of
Jesus's birth. Later, around A.D. 52/53, such mass crucifixions took place again under the Syrian governor Quadratus.
Josephus writes about the procurator Felix (A.D. 52–60):
'The number of robbers he had crucified and of inhabitants
whose connection with the robbers could be proved and who
were similarly punished, rose to terrible proportions.'

The Jews abhorred this form of capital punishment. The
word 'crucify' (*tselov* in talmudic and modern Hebrew) and
the penalty itself were unknown in the Old Testament. The
rule (Deuteronomy 21.22–3) said: 'If a man has committed a
crime punishable by death . . . and you hang him on a tree,
his body shall not remain all night . . .' Hanging a man on a
tree or a pole (Hebrew: *taloh*) after he has been put to death
by stoning, decapitation, etc., must not be confused with
hanging a living body on a cross. Rabbinical literature,
therefore, makes a distinction between hanging on a tree in
the sense of Deuteronomy and 'hanging in the manner of the
(Roman) government'. Crucifixion was not a Jewish punishment, and in no account of the horrors of the Jewish war is it
ever related that the—otherwise not notably gentle—Jewish
rebels crucified their enemies. The one exception was the
crucifixion of 800 rebellious Pharisees by the Maccabean
king Alexander Janaeus (103–76 B.C.). The accounts of that
event—a passage from Josephus and probably also a text
from Qumran—illustrate clearly how harshly the contemporary Jews condemned such an un-Jewish deed.

Although crucifixion was not a Jewish form of capital
punishment, so many of the Jews of Palestine met with it, that
later in the Talmud strict customs and laws regarding it were
established. According to an old Jewish custom, a condemned man was given an anaesthetizing drink (wine and
spices) before his execution, and the Talmud says 'the good
women of Jerusalem' performed this charitable act. When
crucifixions became frequent in Judaea, those condemned to
the cross were presumably also offered such a potion. The
Talmud further relates that the 'good women of Jerusalem'
on the receipt of a bribe were occasionally able to save a man

already hanging on the cross. The nails used for crucifixion were regarded as remedies for a number of illnesses, and the Talmud contains rules regarding this. These nails were therefore even allowed to be worn on the sabbath. Since the crucified frequently remained alive for days, the fact that someone had been seen on a cross was not regarded as incontrovertible evidence of his death. It was possible that he had been taken off the cross before he was dead, through the intercession of friends or the bribing of charitable women. This created problems for the Jewish marriage laws. According to the Talmud, the wife of a crucified man was only able to remarry if the death of her crucified husband had been established or if he had agreed to divorce while on the cross. Crucifixion, quite apart from Christ's crucifixion, has become highly charged emotionally, not only for Christians, but for Jews as well. This explains the stir it caused when in 1968 the remains of a crucified man were found in Jerusalem.

iii *Jehohanan ben Hagqol, the Crucified Man*

During work executed on behalf of the Israeli Ministry of Housing in June 1968, an extensive Jewish burial ground, dating from the period of the second temple, was discovered in the northern part of Jerusalem. At the request of the Department of Museums and Antiquities, several of the burial chambers were opened and examined. This was the first time that the remains of a crucified man, dating from Roman times, were found in an ossuary. The name found scratched into the ossuary was Jehohanan (Aramaic for John), son of Hagqol. This patronymic is not easily explicable; it may be a bowdlerization of 'Ezekiel', or even the rendering of a foreign name. Anatomical examination of the thirty-five skeletons found in the burial chambers which were opened showed that five people had evidently died by violence and three children had starved to death. After all that has already been said about conditions in Judaea in the decades between Herod the Great and the destruction of Jerusalem, this tragic toll is hardly surprising.

Jehohanan ben Hagqol was a contemporary of Jesus. Examination of the remains of his skeleton provided the following clues: Jehohanan was a man aged between twenty-four and twenty-eight years and about five foot six inches tall. He had never done any heavy labour and, since his remains were buried in an ossuary rather than a common bone grave, he had probably belonged to a wealthy family. During his short life he had apparently never suffered a serious illness, but the asymmetrical formation of his head (plagiocephaly and cleft palate) indicate that in the first few weeks of his mother's pregnancy and later, shortly before or during his birth, his life had been threatened by traumatic events. Exact measurements of his cranium made it possible to reconstruct his facial traits. The clue to his violent death by crucifixion was provided by the fact that his feet had been pressed one on the other and fastened to a cross at the heels (*calcaneum*) with a nail five or six inches long and a partially preserved piece of acacia wood. Chemical examination of the bent tip of the nail showed that the cross had been of olive wood. The nails which had fastened the arms were not found, but examination of the bone of the left forearm (between radius and cubitus) showed traces of a nail. The shin of the left leg had been broken, probably by the blow of a club, and, presumably as a consequence of that, both bones of the right lower thigh had broken on the hard edge of the cross. Based on these and other indications, the probable position of the body on the cross could be reconstructed. It appears that when he was taken from the cross, his feet had to be amputated by a hatchet blow, probably because the bent point of the nail had got stuck in a knot in the wood.

Based on these data, and the works of Josephus, it would be easy for a writer of imagination to write a historical novel about Jehohanan's life and even to end it with a passion story. Yet such a novel could never be a gospel. This contemporary of Christ's, looking down on us from the cross, confronts us with the stark reality of crucifixion, but he does not help us to recognize this reality as a message of joy, a victory over the forces of darkness, a turning point in the history of mankind, or as an event of eternal significance. We now possess more exact data about the person of Jehohanan and about his death than we shall ever know about the person and death of Jesus. Yet that which made Christ's life and death a force which created history and, according to

Christian faith, the precondition for our salvation, in Jehohanan's case remains in complete darkness.

2 The Crucifixion of Jesus: Truth and Legend

Jesus of Nazareth was crucified under Pontius Pilate—this is a fact which no one can doubt unless he wilfully ignores all biblical and non-biblical accounts that have come to us. Opinions about the circumstances and reasons of his crucifixion, however, vary considerably. Even in the New Testament there is no unanimity with regard to this question.

i Conflicting Opinions

Was the crucifixion of Jesus the martyrdom of a revolutionary, like that of the Zealots? This interpretation has been put forward at various times since the eighteenth century and has certainly regained currency recently.

Or did the crucifixion take place as described in the much-read book, *The Passover Plot*? According to this, Jesus, imbued with the conviction of his messianic mission, plotted his crucifixion and resurrection. He had himself anaesthetized on the cross by prior agreement, was taken from the cross for dead, and 'buried' by his accomplice, Joseph of Arimathea, and was thus able to appear to his disciples as the risen Jesus. Today there are quite a number of such hypothetical books, some quite solidly based on history. But their authors usually begin with a number of unproven premises and with their help seek to prove what actually happened on the cross; what Jesus, and the people around the cross, thought, planned, and felt. The intention is a full reconstruction of the event, purged of all omissions, alterations, or additions made by the Evangelists for reasons of theology or apologia.

This kind of 'correction' of the Gospels had already begun at the turn of the first century A.D. Ignatius, at the beginning of the second century, thus wrote about Christ's death to the people of Smyrna as follows: 'All this he suffered for our sakes, in order that we might be saved; and he truly suffered, just as he was truly resurrected and not just seemingly, as some unbelievers claim. . . .' The heresy that Christ was only

seemingly dead was proclaimed around A.D. 130–140, particularly by Basilides, a gnostic teacher at Alexandria. He
declared that Christ, the Spirit incarnate sent into the world
by the Father, 'did not suffer, but that instead a certain Simon
of Cyrene was forced to bear the cross for him. This man was
erroneously and unwittingly crucified, having been transformed into Jesus and been taken for him by the executioners. Jesus had taken on the guise of Simon, and ridiculed them
as he looked on.'

The Gospel of Peter, which probably had its origins a little
time later in Syria, relates the events of the crucifixion in a
way similar to the four canonic Gospels. Certain central
aspects of the events and their significance are, however,
modified in a way more indicative of a gnostic view of Jesus.
'He (Jesus) was silent, as if he felt no pain. . . . And the Lord
cried in anguish and called: "My strength, oh strength, thou
hast forsaken me!" And when he had thus spoken, he was
received.' Such accounts and interpretations are no mere
historical curiosities. In Sura 4 of the Koran, the Jews are
accused because 'they said, "We have killed Jesus Christ, the
son of Mary and emissary of God." But (in reality) they did
not kill him (nor) crucify him. (Another) appeared to them in
his guise (so that they took him for Jesus and killed him). . . .
God raised him up (into Heaven).' This is why more than 200
million Muslims today believe what Basilides taught, and
what was borne out by the Gospel of Peter.

As far as speculations as to the course of events of the
crucifixion are concerned, exegesis takes two different view-
points. One school of thought maintains that the only thing
of importance for the faith is Christ's crucifixion as such. It is
not denied that certain details in the accounts of the crucifixion may indeed be based on historical fact, and eyewitnesses
are even cited, such as Simon of Cyrene and the women
present at the crucifixion. But according to this exegesis, even
the events that could actually have happened, such as the
division of the garments, might equally be interpreted as
narrative confirming the Scriptures (thus Mark 15.24 could
be explained by Psalm 22.19). Even where we are given
historically correct details, these are important only in so far
as they serve some apologetic intent or provide some theolog-

ical emphasis. Thus, it would be irrelevant to read the accounts of the crucifixion as historical reports. Rather, they ought to be read and understood as Christian preaching, catechesis, or religious legend. St Paul is invoked as witness for this point of view, because he emphatically stated: 'From now on, therefore, we regard no one from a human point of view; even though we once regarded Christ from a human point of view, we regard him thus no longer.' (2 Cor. 5.16). Thus, Paul was not interested in the details of the crucifixion, but had related and interpreted only the event *as such*.

The other group believe that, although factual reconstruction of the events of the crucifixion, based on biblical sources, would be difficult, it should not be regarded as *a priori* hopeless or immaterial. In contrast to the first group, they are not only interested in the crucifixion *as such*, but also in the *how* and *why*, and wish to examine the historical and factual links between what is historically provable about the crucifixion and the later Christian message.

Is it desirable and possible to reconstruct the event of Jesus's crucifixion? Before we can form a view, a few observations are necessary regarding the available sources.

ii *Biased Sources*

Non-biblical sources regarding the crucifixion are of a late date and do not help in the reconstruction and interpretation of the event. The most valuable non-biblical source is a casual aside in the *Annals* of the Roman historian Tacitus. He explains whence the Christians, whom the Emperor Nero persecuted, took their name: 'The name is derived from Christus, who, in the reign of Tiberius, was condemned to death by the procurator Pontius Pilate. For a while his pernicious superstition was suppressed. But it soon broke out again, not only in Judaea where it had its unfortunate origins, but also in Rome where all that is disgusting, terrible, and shameful is gathered from everywhere and finds its followers.' Apart from the fact that Jesus had been put to death in Judaea by the Romans and an indication as to how an educated Roman outsider saw the event, there is nothing further to be gleaned from this second century source. The frequently quoted passage from Josephus's *Jewish Anti-*

quities, the *Testimonium Flavium*, in its extant version, has been subjected to such thorough Christian revision that it has lost its value as source material. But even the edited version mentions the crucifixion only in one short sentence: 'When on the accusation of our most notable citizens, Pontius Pilate condemned him to death by crucifixion, the love of those who had been devoted to him, remained undiminished.'

With one exception which will be discussed on p. 25, all *Talmud* passages relating to the life of Jesus are probably no more than either a reflection or a refutation of the Christian prophecy. They must therefore also be excluded as source material. Among the existing fragments of *apocryphal gospels*, only the Gospel of Peter contains a description of the crucifixion, as mentioned above. The Christian account of Pilate (the Gospel of Nicodemus), although based on earlier documents, was written in Greek in 425. How far back the documents it was based on should be dated, is difficult to establish. In the middle of the second century Justin mentions such Acts of Pilate twice. But it is unlikely that these could have been the original version of the Nicodemus Gospel, or indeed a once existing, but now lost, 'protocol' of the trial of Jesus.

Non-biblical sources yield extremely little about the crucifixion. Anyone who wishes to inform himself about the event and the meaning of the crucifixion must therefore turn to the *New Testament*. The hymns and confessions which are part of the oldest Christian traditions, and which are quoted in the Epistles of the New Testament and in the Revelation of John, contain the occasional reference to the passion story. But as regards the crucifixion itself, the emphasis is on the event as such and its theological interpretation (see also pp. 51–3ff). The sermons in the Acts of the Apostles are similar in this. The only New Testament sources which can give us clues as to the *how* and *why*, beyond relating the event *as such*, are the accounts of the crucifixion in the Gospels. The question arises, however, whether these accounts are simply sermons which have taken the form of a narrative and are thus later theological interpretations of the crucifixion, or whether there is a historical and factual connection between the life and message of Jesus and the later Christian message and its various interpretations of the crucifixion. In order to answer this question, it is necessary to be clear about the special nature of these accounts in the Gospels.

3 Memory, Tradition, Interpretation

i Approaching the Event via the Texts

It is true not only for the Gospel of John that 'Jesus did many other signs in the presence of the disciples, which are not written in this book; but these are written that you may believe that Jesus is the Christ, the Son of God, and that believing you may have life in his name' (John 20.30–1). The Gospels are not a chronicle of Jesus's life, nor are they ancient historiography, even though Luke in his foreword (Luke 1.1–4) makes use of the formulae of classical historiography. The Gospels are an account of belief in the risen Lord, intended to awaken faith, or to correct and strengthen it. This faith, according to all four Gospels, is not simply based on the belief of the original Christian community, but on Jesus of Nazareth's deeds, prophecies, and suffering, and in particular on his crucifixion and the certainty of the resurrection of the crucified Christ.

The authors of the Gospels did not doubt that they were relating facts. But for them these events were not merely 'bare facts'; they assumed their significance in the light of the Old Testament and of the Kingdom that was to come. Thus the events they described—and in particular the crucifixion—always point far beyond the mere facts. The crucifixion is seen and told in the context of the story of the Lord and his creation. In this respect there exists a significant difference between biblical and modern attitudes to the understanding of history, as in the latter such all-embracing points of reference are absent. The statement that attitudes to history differed should not lead us to the assumption that at the time of Jesus there existed no interest in history. Not only did such interest exist in the centuries following Christ, but there were also copious instructions as to how history should be examined and written. The Gospel writers, however, were not schooled in this critical method, as were Justin and especially Origen. Even Luke, although his intention was to write history, wrote a Gospel—a particular and quite novel literary form. But does this mean that the authors of the Gospels were not interested in the life of Jesus and that it is therefore not possible to use them in order to retrace Jesus's life and death?

Form-critical exegesis has endeavoured to retrace history through the traditions which were assimilated in the Gospels back to the very origins of those traditions, and thus to determine how and when their various stages and categories came into being. According to this research, the oldest traditions are not historical accounts, even though they may contain genuine sayings of Jesus and eyewitness accounts.

'All form-critical research is predicated upon the fact that the history of traditions does not originate in historical reporting, but in a narrative that has its source in faith and in the intention to awaken faith.' This statement by one of the founding fathers of form criticism may be correct, but it immediately prompts the further question: how did this tradition come into existence?

Form-critical exegesis answers this by referring to the original Christian community who worshipped Christ and proclaimed, taught, and defended its faith in him. But in this it seems to trust the community's theological creativity more than its capacity to remember the teachings and the passion of Jesus.

ii *Approaching the Texts via the Event*

Can one supplement what form criticism has achieved in retracing the path from the Gospels to the oldest traditions, by examining the development from the teaching and suffering Christ, via oral and written traditions, to the present text of the Gospels? This question has been answered affirmatively, particularly by Swedish students of the New Testament.

Briefly summarized, their thesis runs as follows. The traditions of the New Testament had their origin in a period and in a climate where there existed quite specific methods of transmission and tradition. The study of ancient teaching methods, as they can be observed in rabbinical Judaism and also in the Greek schools of philosophy—and which were probably also adopted by Jesus and the apostles—leads to the following proposition: in the beginning was not the original Christian sermon, but Jesus of Nazareth who instructed by word and deed. Just as he instructed his disciples in the Lord's Prayer, he also committed his entire message to their memory. Given the ancient scepticism towards the written word, this was a primarily oral tradition, which did not transmit texts, but the firmly established *Evangelium Jesu Christi* (i.e. the good news of and about Jesus Christ), together with interpretations by the various teachers. Therefore, the Christian tradition did *not* originate in a diffuse way through an anonymous, theologically creative first generation of Christians who then, according to their various 'stations in life', variously transmitted and changed it by idiosyncratic redaction. On the contrary, from the beginning, there existed the College of Twelve in Jerusalem and authorized bearers of gospel tradition throughout the Church, who supervised the process of the creation of tradition and its transmission. It was not solely a question of transmission, but also of constant work on and with the 'Words of the Lord'. The Old Testament was interpreted in the light of the gospel. In answer to new questions of faith and the life of the Church, new teachings and deeds of Christ were added to the tradition from memory and interpreted. When the Gospels had to be written down—as an emergency measure, as it were—they were not only based on the actual memories of the bearers of tradition, but also on already existing notes, treatises, and collections of documents that had been assembled for various purposes.

This hypothesis, which has been put forward with immense scholarliness and copious source material, must be taken seriously. In my view, it is worth noting the following conclusions, not all of which, by the way, stem from the above hypothesis:

(1) A great many of the traditions of the New Testament have their point of origin in the teaching, the life, and the passion of Jesus of Nazareth; thus there exists a significant

historical and factual continuity between Jesus of Nazareth
and the message of the Christ.

(2) The remembrance of Jesus played an important role,
not only in the creation of tradition, but also later in its
transmission and interpretation.

(3) From the beginning the Church had its universally
recognized bearers of tradition. Whether they can be called
'teaching authorities', in the light of somewhat ambiguous
testimony in this respect in the New Testament, is questionable; but there is no doubt that they played an
important part in the creation and transmission of tradition.

(4) During roughly the first century of church history, it is
quite probable that in some locally confined churches and
schools the oral traditions of the Gospels were transmitted
in the manner suggested by the above hypothesis.

Despite areas of agreement on relevant points, the above
hypothesis remains unsatisfactory for the following reasons:

(1) The picture of Jesus, who commits his teachings to the
memory of his disciples and supervises the proper learning of
them by heart, ill accords with the picture of him which we
gain from the Gospels. Even though one could obviously
point here to the symbolic act of washing feet, where Jesus
consciously established a didactic model, Christ's deeds and
suffering are much more than just didactic models to be
imitated by his disciples. His obedience on the way to the
cross and his call to follow him are not the same as a didactic,
symbolic act and a call to imitate him. Jesus was not only the
powerful teacher, but also the prophet empowered by the
Spirit, and beyond that 'the man who exploded all models of
thought'. The story and person of Christ have the 'character
of the immediately present'. It was because of this constantly
new and astonishing nature of his presence—and not by
some technique of memorizing—that his words and deeds
and his passion impressed themselves on the memory of his
disciples.

(2) If the process of creating and transmitting the tradition
had occurred in the manner assumed in the above hypothesis,
it would be very difficult to explain how, in a matter of a few

decades, such a great—and sometimes conflicting—variety of gospel traditions could have sprung up. In this context we have not only to consider the traditions assembled in the canon of the New Testament, but must give thought as well to the origins of the 'other gospels' of Paul's adversaries, to the 'apocryphal' gospels, etc. It is obvious that, apart from the recollection and witness of the 'official' bearers of tradition, other sources and persons must have been at work.

(3) In the above hypothesis, the main significance is placed on Christ's words, while his deeds, and particularly his passion, are relegated to secondary importance, because they impressed themselves on the memory of his disciples as models and thus the description of his deeds and his passion does not stem from Jesus himself, but from the community. Collections of Jesus's words indeed existed early on, but it is significant that the Gospels which have been incorporated into the canon of the New Testament, are those that were written with the emphasis on the passion and the resurrection. In them, the word is not preferred above the deed, nor the teachings above the way to the cross. The above hypothesis serves to explain the origins and method of transmission of certain rabbinical writings, such as the Mishnic tractate *Aboth*, or certain apocryphal Christian manuscripts, such as the gnostic gospel of Thomas. These almost exclusively contain 'words'. But with regard to the later, canonically recognized, gospel traditions, the above hypothesis does not cover the central issue.

iii *The Origin of Tradition*

Can the valid insights which form-critical studies have gained for us be combined with the valid conclusions from the hypothesis which we discussed above? In my view this seems entirely possible, and here follows an attempt to do so.

The remembrance of the teachings, the life, and the death of Christ remained alive, because Christ's constantly new and amazing presence and power—which I described above—had impressed themselves on the minds of his disciples. It has often been maintained that the first generation Church had been so imbued with the presence of the risen Lord and the expectation of his imminent return, that these memories played a very minor role. It would be more justifiable to assume that precisely because the Church believed in the risen Lord and expected his return, it kept his memory alive. However, this had little to do with keeping it alive for the archives. It did not lead to the writing of a chronicle or biography of Jesus, nor did it develop directly into the traditions of the Gospels. It remained rather as a reservoir and a corrective for the creation and transmission of tradition. In several cases, a certain tension between memory and tradition can be observed. The memory influenced tradition, but conversely tradition slowly began to put its stamp on memory. Thus memory cannot be considered to be historically exact.

The following factors played an important part in the formation of the Gospel traditions. First of all it seems that geographical locations, and therefore cultural differences, were important. Differing traditions were obviously developed in Jerusalem and Judaea, in Galilee and western Syria, in Edessa and eastern Syria, in the countries around the Aegean, in Egypt, or in Rome; they were influenced and interpreted according to differing images of Jesus and varying testimonies. Differences in traditions were also caused by differing groups of eyewitnesses and other accounts. In addition, traditions were developed for specific ends within the life and mission of the Church: for worship, catechesis, and missionary purposes. Finally, some of the traditions were formed simply by oral transmission and the passing on of memories, without any of the above factors coming into play.

The formation of tradition also came about partially on an unconscious level, by the adaptation of memories to existing narrative styles and existing notions of the nature of the divine in a specific cultural context. But closely linked to this, conscious *interpretation* played a decisive part. This can be observed in the Epistles of Paul and in the work of redaction performed by the writers of the Gospels. Before them it had been largely the Christian prophets who had fulfilled the function of tradition-creating interpretation. These interpretations not only involved a conscious choice in the selection of this or that element from the store of memory, they also answered concrete questions of the day, within a specific cultural context, by pointing out the meaning of remembered words or deeds. In this, theological, apologetic, pastoral, and missionary motives came into play. Beyond that, the process of interpretation brought forth 'words' which had not been spoken by Jesus and 'events' which had not happened to him in his lifetime. This can be particularly observed in the narration of the crucifixion in the Gospels.

But there were limits to this kind of theological creativity. On the one hand, form-critical studies have shown that quite early on the story of Jesus assumed very definite forms of oral and written tradition and that these tended to be 'conservative'. On the other hand, the memory of Jesus remained vivid for a long time through oral transmission, even after the traditions began to be cast in written form. In the first half of the second century, Papias continued to prefer oral traditions, wherever they were available to him; and from a letter dating towards the end of that century, written by Irenaeus to Flavius, a former fellow student, we know that even shortly before A.D. 200 there still existed memories of Jesus which had been passed on by word of mouth. For a long time, therefore, interpretation was not confined only to the meaning of fixed written or oral gospel traditions, but also remained interpretation of remembered words and deeds, of the passion and death of Jesus of Nazareth, the now risen and spiritually present Lord. Relatively late traditions, therefore, can sometimes encapsulate a better historical memory than the very early ones.

It has generally been assumed that from the beginning there has been only *one* image of Jesus (that of the crucified and risen Lord), *one* original message (such as the apostolic sermon in the Acts) and equally only *one* central creed (such as 1 Cor. 15.3ff). Heresy would thus be understood simply as any deviation from this original and correct tradition of faith. Form-critical studies of the New Testament, as well as studies of the history of the redaction of the gospel, however, point to an immense theological multiplicity. There has not been the direct development from the life and death of Christ towards a rightly believing Church, which has usually been assumed. It would be more correct to speak of the 'lines of development' of early Christianity. Thus, in the beginning there was no creed but Jesus of Nazareth. The memory of him, however, did not constitute an unequivocal point of departure for a unified Christian theology, as Jesus evoked differing images. According to one interesting hypothesis, there were originally four different categories of gospel:

(1) The collections of sayings; notably the *logia* source used by Matthew and Luke, but also the entire line of development that culminated in the Thomas gospel with its 114 *logia*.

(2) The gospels of Jesus as the Divine Man (*Aretalogia*); to this category also belongs the possible collection of miracles Jesus performed, as well as the message of Paul's adversaries in the second Epistle to the Corinthians and the later apocryphal gospels of the infancy of Christ.

(3) Gospels as revelations, which are not only contained in the apocalypses, teachings, and revelations to the disciples of the now canonical Gospels, but also in much later gnostic 'gospels' and 'revelations'.

(4) The Gospels containing the story of the passion and resurrection, into which the above three other categories of gospel have been incorporated but also reinterpreted in the light of a central profession of faith in the crucified and resurrected Lord. Only this fourth category of Gospel was admitted into the canon of the New Testament. According to the judgement of the Church, Christ's words, miracles, and revelations were not to be separated from his death and resurrection.

The assumptions regarding the canonic Gospels, outlined above, will certainly not be the last word on the subject. There is no doubt that the memory of the crucifixion, and by no means only the memory of the event *as such*, played a major part in them. It therefore enables us to make an attempt to reconstruct the event.

4 *Crucified under Pontius Pilate*

The passion stories in the Gospels are neither historical accounts of what really happened, nor merely a theological interpretation of Christ's death in the manner of a narrative sermon as, say, Psalm 22. These accounts are rather interpretations of the remembered crucifixion. It is therefore not possible to understand them correctly if one sees them only as the exact reconstruction of what happened at the crucifixion, or only as a theological reflection.

i   *Reconstruction of Events*

Based on the accounts in the Gospels, and on what is known from non-biblical sources about crucifixions in Palestine at the time, it is possible to describe the probable course of events. In this regard historians are usually less sceptical than theologians. Whether the details of what occurred are to be considered certainties, probabilities, or improbabilities must remain a matter of judgement. The case is similar with regard to those elements which are considered with certainty—or at least some probability—to be later interpretations by the early Christians. It will also be shown later that differentiation between actual occurrences and 'mere' interpretations is dubious, and while a distinction between the two can be drawn, they must not be divorced from each other.

The fact that Jesus of Nazareth was crucified, cruelly suffered, and then died under Pontius Pilate is, in my view, a certainty. It is also to be considered certain that a man by the name of Simon of Cyrene, the father of Alexander and Rufus, was forced to carry the transverse bar, at least for part of the way. To me it seems certain, furthermore, that Jesus was crucified between two 'robbers' who probably were rebels, after having been condemned to death as a political suspect by the prefect Pilate.

The most difficult question to answer regarding Christ's trial (or trials) falls outside the scope of this present essay. It is nevertheless necessary to point out the historical problem in this connection: the Gospels do not depict Jesus as a religio-political rebel. His all-powerful teachings and deeds did not bring him into conflict with the Roman administration, but with the Jewish authorities. The Jewish trial—if indeed it took place—therefore charged Jesus with blasphemy (Mark 14.64). But why then was he not stoned? These stonings did occur at the time of the New Testament, although the Sanhedrin was no longer authorized to decide about the life or death of an accused. The best known example of this is the account of the stoning of Stephen in Acts 7.54–60. But the Gospels also relate that Jesus was threatened with stoning and with the related punishment of being thrown headlong from the brow of a hill (John 8.59; 10.31–3; 11.8; Luke 4.28–30). Josephus reports further, in a credible passage, that James, the brother of Jesus, was stoned, together with other Christians. An old Talmud text, which probably contains historical memories independent of Christian sources, relates: 'On the eve of the Feast of Passover, Jesus (the Nazarene) was hanged. For forty days the crier preceded him: "Jesus of Nazareth is to be stoned because he has committed sorcery, enticed Israel, and drawn her away! Whosoever knows of acquittal for him should come forth and speak for him!" But no acquittal was found for him and he was hanged on the eve of Passover.' Two of the charges in this Talmud text, 'to entice' and 'to draw away', use exactly the same Hebrew concepts as in Deut. 13.1–11. The charges are clearly linked to blasphemy and also recall Mark 3.22. The sentence of stoning was thus justified according to Jewish law. Whether 'hanging' refers to Deut. 21.22 or to the Roman crucifixion remains uncertain.

Jesus was not stoned, he was crucified. The historical problem posed thereby can be solved in different ways. Some people maintain, for instance, that the accounts in the Gospels are extremely tendentious; they see the tensions between Jesus and the Jewish authorities essentially as a projection of the later disputes between the Church and rabbinical Jewry, and assume that no Jewish trial took place; they regard Jesus essentially as a rebel who was condemned to crucifixion. Others emphasize the Jewish condemnation as the dramatic climax of the conflict of power between Jesus and the Jewish authorities; in this, however, they minimize the fact that it was the Romans who sentenced and crucified Jesus. Both attempts at a solution are unsatisfactory. The problem remains. The life and actions of Jesus obviously led him not only into conflict with the Jewish elders (and therefore potentially to stoning) but also to the trial by Pilate and thus indeed to crucifixion. One thing is clear: in the situation of Palestine at that time, religious and political aspects were inseparable one from the other.

The crucifixion of Jesus probably took place at Golgotha. This place is usually identified as being the outcrop of rock several yards high at the edge of a quarry which had been exploited before the Babylonian exile. It lies to the north-west, outside the second ring of city walls of the old Jerusalem, where today stands the church of the Holy Sepulchre. Whether Jesus was led to this place of execution from the Antonian castle north of the Temple or from the palace of Herod to the south, is difficult to determine. Since the fourteenth century the traditional *via dolorosa* has led from the Antonian castle to Golgotha, but it is probable that the way to the cross began at Herod's palace.

It is even more difficult to determine when Jesus was crucified. It is well known that the Synoptics and John contradict each other in this matter. According to the synoptic Gospels, Jesus died on a Passover day, that is to say on Friday, 15 Nisan, at three o'clock in the afternoon. According to John, the crucifixion took place in the late afternoon on the eve of Passover on Friday, 14 Nisan. In the synoptic Gospels, as well as in John's, the chronology of the passion is partly determined by theological motives. The Synoptists interpret the last supper as a Passover meal, hence probably 15 Nisan. John was in all likelihood intent on synchronizing the death of Jesus with the hour when Passover lambs were slaughtered, hence probably 14 Nisan, even though it remains uncertain whether John really regarded Jesus as a Passover lamb. Several attempts have been made to harmonize the synoptic accounts with that of John, by assuming that two different calendars or two different methods to calculate the time of day had been used. Had the official Jewish calendar, based on the moon year, or an old priestly calendar, based on the sun year, been used—or indeed both in conjunction? There is also the open question in what year 14 or 15 Nisan would have fallen on a Friday. This is a complex astronomical problem, because it has to be decided whether in A.D. 30 on a certain evening in March or April atmospheric conditions in Jerusalem were such as to allow the new moon to be visible. In any case, in A.D. 28, 29 and 32 neither 14 nor 15 Nisan could have been on a Friday. If the year 31 was a leap year and, because of clouds, the new moon was seen a day late, thus putting back the beginning of the month by one day, it is possible that Christ was crucified on 15 Nisan (27 April) of A.D. 31. It is much more probable, though, that Jesus died on Friday, 14 Nisan (7 April) in A.D. 30.

As far as the further course of the crucifixion is concerned, it seems to me entirely possible that the Roman soldiers, who had been charged with the execution, divided Christ's (and probably also the two rebels') garments among themselves and that, according to Jewish custom, the condemned was offered an anaesthetizing drink. The account that a tablet, giving the reason for Jesus's conviction, was fastened to the cross may also be based on quite authentic memory, although this is frequently disputed. It is probable that, as usual, curious onlookers followed the condemned to his place of execution, as well as several of the women who had attached themselves to the circle of Christ's disciples. It may also be assumed that during the crucifixion, the soldiers, at least, mocked Jesus. The possibility that Jesus spoke to the onlookers on the way to and during his crucifixion can also not be excluded. It is highly probable that he died with astonishing quickness, uttering a cry. The account that the centurion voiced his amazement about this rapid death may be based on solid recollection. It is certainly to be assumed that a military guard was placed on the site of execution until the three condemned were dead.

Many details of the crucifixion remain uncertain. For instance, we do not know what kind of cross was used, what the exact medical cause of death was, nor even whether Jesus was tied or nailed to the cross. The only account of the crucifixion which refers to the use of nails is the Gospel of Peter, although it can be deduced also from John 20.25, 27 that during the second half of the first century the Church of John, probably correctly, assumed Jesus had been nailed to the cross (cf. Luke 24.39).

It remains difficult to determine whether Jesus, before dying, did indeed utter the beginning of Psalm 22, as related by Mark and Matthew, but not by Luke and John. It is unlikely that the Christian community would otherwise have attributed to Jesus this cry of god-forsakenness, and it is true that Jews frequently recited psalms in their hour of death. This may be an indication that this detail was based on historical recollection. Against the historical validity of it can be argued that the entire account of the crucifixion is strongly coloured by Psalm 22. The other words Jesus is reported to have spoken on the cross have their probable origin in later interpretations of his death. The rending of the temple curtains, the earthquake, the rising of the dead, and probably also the sudden darkness are almost certainly interpretations by early Christians.

The distinction made in the above paragraphs between probable events and probable interpretations is tentative. It is certainly possible to place different emphases here and there. But more important is the question whether the attempted distinction between events and interpretation is applicable to biblical modes of thought.

ii Is Distinction between Event and Interpretation Relevant?

Even if the distinction is maintained—which is largely the case in the present study—it must be stated forthwith that the events related in the Bible are unique. This is particularly apparent in the case of the crucifixion. It is possible to relate the death of Jesus as one would report the crucifixion of Jehohanan ben Hagqol, and thus to elicit human compassion or archaeological interest. Yet the biblical accounts of the crucifixion are quite different. Through them all runs the certainty that, though Jesus was executed in a manner similar to the crucifixion of the two rebels beside him, he was nevertheless the Lord with the power to teach and to act, who became the risen and ever-present Christ. His crucifixion is thus odd, repugnant, and illogical. Only those who seek to see Jesus on the cross in isolation from all other knowledge which we have about his life and his deeds, and about his later influence on world history, object to the factual accounts of the crucifixion in the Scriptures being imbued with so much interpretation of the event.

These interpretations—even including the apocalyptic descriptions of natural phenomena—are perfectly relevant to the curious event of Christ's crucifixion. It is not only later interpretation which lends weight and meaning to the crucifixion, but the strangeness of the event itself. Not only did it happen, but it was also deeply significant. It is therefore not possible to understand the crucifixion properly, by paying attention either only to actual events or only to interpretations, or by simply maintaining that biblical facts are 'actual facts mingled with interpretation'. The case is rather that biblical facts are portentous events unfolded by interpretation.

This statement leads to an insight which makes any clear distinction between actual events and later interpretation questionable. Historical events are open to the future. Their importance will continue to unfold. Constant interpretation therefore properly belongs to the account of events, and the sharp distinction made by modern Western thought between event and interpretation is inadequate in dealing with the open-endedness of historical events. What is being done, thought, or omitted now, influences not only the future but past events as well. It can lend another meaning to 'historical facts', give them more or less importance, put them into a new context, call them into being or abolish them altogether. This or that fact is picked from the store of recollection, or consigned to oblivion. Such open-endedness applies to all history, but biblical thought gives it particular emphasis, because it is consciously directed towards the End (the Kingdom of God), and is also judged from the viewpoint of this End. The event of the crucifixion is still 'unfinished', because it is constantly reinterpreted from a new situation and from the point of view of the hoped-for End.

This chapter about the crucifixion itself must therefore not be separated from the ensuing chapters which deal with the New Testament interpretations of the crucifixion. Not only the general open-endedness of history, but the strangely significant nature of Jesus's crucifixion, lead us straight into an ongoing interpretation of this event.

29

2
The Earliest Traditions of the Crucifixion

Which came first, the pre-canonic 'confessions' and hymns about Jesus's death and resurrection, or the pre-canonic narrative of the passion? This is the subject of an old dispute. Most scholars give priority to the pre-Pauline confessions. Yet, if the remarks about 'memories, traditions, and interpretation' (pp. 16–23ff) have described the process of the creation of tradition more or less accurately, there can be no simple answer to the above question. We must assume that for differing situations and for different purposes manifold traditions were developed simultaneously. One thing can, however, be stated with certainty: the earliest *book* about the passion is the Old Testament.

1 *The Perception of Death: the Suffering Righteous One*

When the Emmaus disciples went home in disappointment and assumed the crucifixion to have been the ignominious end of the story of Jesus, the risen Christ showed them that 'beginning with Moses and all the prophets . . . (it was) necessary that Christ should suffer these things and enter into his glory' (Luke 24.25–7).

There is no need at this point to go into how the encounter with the risen Christ actually happened. The account of the Emmaus disciples is a parable of what happened after the crucifixion. The disciples and Jesus's other followers were obviously deeply shaken by his death. But when they became certain that the crucified Jesus had risen from the dead and was present, they began to ponder the significance of the apparently senseless crucifixion. They recalled certain of Jesus's sayings, deeds, and attitudes before his death. But more particularly, they tried to obtain an interpretation of the events from Scripture. The risen one himself opened their eyes through the Holy Spirit, through the prophets, teachers, and exegetic schools. In this way they discovered the Old Testament anew.

i The 'Bible of the early Church'

It is frequently assumed that the authors of the New Testament had at their disposal a finished, written source containing the Old Testament texts which prophesied or bore witness to the coming of a Messiah. The early Christians probably knew all the texts which had been incorporated into the Hebrew Old Testament. Beyond that, they read some of the intertestamental books of wisdom and apocalyptic texts which, in part, belonged to the canon of the Septuagint, the Greek translation of the Old Testament. From this a series of 'key texts' were gradually evolved, which explained the significance of Christ's life, teaching, death, and resurrection.

The 'Bible of the early Church' contained: (1) apocalyptic-eschatological passages, (2) prophecies about the people of Israel and their future, (3) psalms about the suffering righteous and 'servant songs', as well as (4) a number of texts which cannot be subsumed under any general heading.

Primary Texts	Secondary Texts
(1) Joel 2—3; Zechariah 9—14; Daniel 7	Malachi 3.1–6; Daniel 12
(2) Hosea; Isaiah 6.1—9.7; 11.1–10; 28.16; 40.1–11; Jeremiah 31.10–34	Isaiah 29.9–14; Jeremiah 7.1–15; Habakkuk 1—2
(3) Isaiah 42.1—44. 5; 49.1–13; 50.4–11; 52.13—53.12; 61; Psalms 22; 31; 34; 38; 41; 42–43; 69; 80; 88; 118	Isaiah 58.6–10
(4) Psalms 2; 8; 110 Genesis 12.3; 22.18; Deuteronomy 18.15; 19	Psalms 16; 132; 2 Samuel 7.13–14; Isaiah 55.3; Amos 9.11–12

At the time when Christian traditions were formed, the canon of the Old Testament was not yet complete. To the above list, texts and passages from intertestamental sources would thus have to be added. But more important is the fact that, at the time of Jesus, the texts of the Old Testament were read and comprehended through the prism, as it were, of intertestamental literature. It is difficult to determine with precision, at what point in the creation of tradition the use of which Old Testament or intertestamental source as 'key texts' should be fixed. It is equally uncertain which parts of the Scriptures were used by Jesus of Nazareth himself. But we *can* say that the study of how the first Christians used the Scriptures furnishes some insight into the period when tradition was formed, and therefore also into the initial stages of the theological interpretation of Christ's death.

Paul, Mark, Matthew, Luke, and John made different selections from the Scriptures and employed somewhat different methods of biblical interpretation. What they have in common, however, is the certainty that in the life, death, and resurrection of Jesus something of eschatological significance had occurred. In contrast to contemporary historical exegesis, they did not take as their starting point the biblical texts and their literary and historical origins in order to interpret the significance of such texts for a new situation. For them the starting point was a contemporary event—in this case the crucifixion—which had to be interpreted in the light of existing key texts. The interpretation of biblical texts was by no means an invention of the first Christians. The Qumran sect had interpreted in a similar manner, as was made evident when the 'Habakkuk commentary' was found in the Qumran library. This commentary is an explanation of the book of Habakkuk which, in the light of miraculous events experienced by the Qumranites, made topical and partly modified the Habakkuk text.

The first Christians, in their reflection on Scripture, frequently followed a similar course, though in a far less methodical fashion than the Qumran sect. They read the Old Testament and made it topical, in the light of Christ's death and resurrection, and collected key texts from the Old Testament and intertestamental sources for the understanding and the defence of their faith.

It is highly likely that this use of the Old Testament began in connection with the interpretation of the repugnant but significant events of Jesus's passion. Thus, the relevant passages from the Old Testament probably constitute the oldest elements of the 'Bible of the early Church' and were probably already playing their part during the third and fourth decades of the first century. The existing Jewish lists of texts containing Messianic prophecies—such as the *Testimonia* and *Florilegia* found in the library of Qumran—were no help. Other passages had to be found. Which then were the texts that played a key role and formed the basis of the interpretation of Christ's death as it entered into the earliest traditions of the crucifixion?

ii *The Gospel of the Passion in the Old Testament*

The above outline of the elements contained in the 'Bible of the early Church' mentions under heading (4) passages from Isaiah and the Psalms which gained particular significance for the interpretation of the crucifixion. To these must be added several apocalyptic-eschatological passages under heading (1), and particularly Zechariah 9—14. In these texts the first Christians discovered the 'gospel of the passion'.

What does this earliest gospel say about the crucifixion of Jesus? This question can only be answered by reference to quotations from the Old Testament and allusions to them in the accounts of the crucifixion in the four Gospels. Chapter 4 will further examine which of these quotations and allusions stem from old traditions and which from redaction of the Gospels.

In the following table the references for actual quotations are set in italic numerals. References not in italics indicate allusions to Old Testament texts, and brackets indicate passages that were probably influenced by the texts listed.

Opinions may differ regarding inclusion or exclusion of this or that passage in the table, or as regards the assessment of their function. But we can properly call quotations only those passages of the crucifixion narrative in the four Gospels where these are rendered in roughly the same terms as in the Hebrew or Septuagint passages of the Old Testament. We would therefore be justified in assuming for Luke 23.49 not only quotation from Ps. 38.11 but also from

Old Testament		Mark	Matt.	Luke	John
Ps. 22.2	('My God . . .')	15.34	27.46	—	—
Ps. 22.7	('All who see me . . .')	—	—	23.35	—
Ps. 22.7	('They wag their heads . . .')	15.29	27.39	—	—
Ps. 22.8	(Trust in God)	—	27.43	—	—
Ps. 22.15	(Thirst)	—	—	—	(19.28)
Ps. 22.18	(Division of Garments)	15.24	27.35	23.34	19.24
Ps. 31.5	('Into Thy Hand . . .')	—	—	23.46	—
Ps. 38.11	(Friends aloof)	15.40	27.55	23.49	—
Ps. 69.21	(Poison)	—	27.34	—	—
Ps. 69.21	(Vinegar)	15.36	27.48	23.36	19.28ff
Isa. 53.12	(2 Robbers)	(15.27)	(27.38)	(23.33)	(19.18)
Dan. 12.2	(The dead awaken)	—	27.52ff	—	—
Hos. 10.8	('Fall upon us . . .')	—	—	23.30	—
Amos 8.9	(Darkness)	15.33	27.45	23.44	—

Ps. 88.8. Perhaps it is a case—as elsewhere in the New Testament—of a compound quotation. Allusions and probable influences are hard to pinpoint, since in the Old Testament the same utterances are repeated frequently. It would therefore be possible to indicate not only Amos 8.9 for a reference to darkness, but also the influence of Isa. 13.9ff; 50.3; and Exod. 10.21ff. Allusions to the intertestamental Book of Wisdom 2.13, 18–20 are to be assumed for Mark 15.39 and Matt. 27.43.

Some remarkable conclusions can be drawn from the above table of quotations. The first thing to note is that in the passion narratives of the four Gospels the 'servant songs', and in particular the passage from Isa. 52.13—53.12 which is always linked with the passion, play no part, or only a very minor one. Mark 15.28 expressly quotes Isa. 53.12, but this v.28 is an insertion from Luke 22.37 which is not contained in the best manuscripts and is thus rightly omitted in most modern translations, or given merely as a footnote. The influence of Isa. 53.12 on Mark 15.27 is very uncertain. Neither this verse, even if it is influenced by Isa. 53.12, nor the quotation in v.28, added later, interpret the death of Jesus as a redemption of man's sins.

The concept of atoning for the sins of others—which is of such importance for the doctrine of redemption—can perhaps be read into the quotation from Ps. 34.22, Exod.

12.46 and Zech. 12.10, contained in the last scenes of John's passion narrative (John 19.36ff). Whether this is as certain as some people maintain will be examined in chapter 4, section 5. At any rate, the passion narratives of the synoptic Gospels do not interpret Jesus's death, by reference to quotations from Scripture, as one of redemption or atonement.

Where then does the theological emphasis lie in these passages from Scripture which refer to very old, and perhaps even the earliest, crucifixion traditions? It is worth noting that the quotations refer almost exclusively to Psalms. What is more, most quotations refer to Psalms 22, 38, and 69 which all belong to the category of songs of lament (and praise). By far the greatest influence was exerted by Psalm 22, which is quoted no less than nine times in the four crucifixion narratives.

iii *Psalm 22 and the Figure of the Suffering Righteous*

Psalm 22 follows the general structure of individual songs of lament and praise: an individual supplicant in his misery addresses himself to God. He is mortally ill, a 'worm' (v.6), his strength is dried up (vv.14 and 15), and his death is near (v.20); he is surrounded by enemies who mock him and take on menacing shapes in his feverish imagination (vv.6–8; 12–13; 16–18; 21). But the worst is that God is far off and has forsaken him (vv.1; 11; 19). His inner and outward suffering is incomprehensible to him. God's absence, silence, and non-intervention does not tally with his own experience or that of his forefathers hitherto. He nevertheless cleaves to God. The cry about his god-forsakenness is followed not only by laments, but also by remembrance of past deliverance and help (vv.3–5; 9–10). The paradoxical insight dawns that it is God Himself who has inflicted this suffering (v.15).

Then follows, as in many songs of lament, the change to a song of praise. Deliverance is celebrated in the temple. The sick man may now praise God in the midst of the congregation (vv.22ff). He assembles the poor for a sacrificial meal in order to rejoice with them (v.26).

How should this change be understood? Did a priest in the temple pronounce an oracle of healing (v.21 might perhaps be interpreted in this way), so that now, in the expectation of being healed, a promise of praise is made? Or is it that the entire psalm is a narrative of lament and praise which is recited during the feast of thanksgiving following deliverance? But it could also be understood that the supplicant in the midst of his afflictions is able to struggle through to the certainty of divine salvation, and that he is thus already able, while still suffering, to praise God and to look forward to the feast of thanksgiving in the temple. Or the recognition suffices—voiced in the third line of verse 15—that God is active even in the midst of his incomprehensible sufferings, so that he can praise him even in the depth of misery.

It is no longer possible to determine how, in the original situation of Psalm 22, the change from lament to praise came about. However, the psalm did not remain the prayer of a single individual. Lament and praise are expressed with such typical imagery that the prayer was soon adopted for the liturgical use of the temple. The supplicant was seen as the paradigm of a sufferer who, although overcome by the most terrible affliction of god-forsakenness, nevertheless experiences God's deliverance.

It is possible that the psalm originally ended with verse 26 and that the praise of verses 27–31 was added later for liturgical use. Now all restraints are abandoned, and not only the original supplicant who has been turned into an archetypal figure of suffering, but with him the entire congregation praises God, as well as 'all the families of the nations', and even the dead (the enigmatic v.29 could perhaps be thus interpreted) and all the coming generations join in. The individual's lonely cry of god-forsakenness finds in the whole world and at all times an echo of praise and faith in the Lord.

Once the psalm was adopted into the liturgical traditions of the people of Israel, and had gained universal and eschatological dimensions through its concluding verses, it is hardly surprising that it was recited time and again. It is for instance to be assumed that Psalm 22 strongly influenced the songs of praise of the Qumran sect. The author of these latter songs identifies with the authors of the psalms of lament and praise, but it is significant that he does not identify with the pattern of promise and fulfilment. He sees the course of the supplicant in these psalms rather as a typical fate—the necessary path for the righteous in God.

The figure of the suffering righteous one plays an important role in Old Testament piety. It probably originated with the figure of the king surrounded by enemies, but delivered by God. Psalm 18 (Ps.18 = 2 Sam.22) is particularly revealing in this respect. It contains a number of allusions to Zion ('rock', 'refuge'). The deliverance of King David from the midst of his enemies was seen as proof of God's faithfulness to those who keep to his ordinance and was recalled as such in the hymns of praise. This was the point of origin of the concept of the suffering, but delivered, righteous man. When the royal forms of prayer were democratized, the archetypal figure of the suffering and delivered righteous one was also recognized in a sick and outcast supplicant such as the subject of Psalm 22. An important development of this Old Testament motif can be recognized in Ps.119. There the enemies are not those who persecute the pious, but the wicked who disregard God and his statutes. Because the supplicant is steadfast in the cause of God he must suffer and thus experience his afflictions not as a temptation of faith, but rather as confirmation of his proper relationship to God. The suffering of the righteous is combined with the suffering of the Lord's poor (cf. Ps.34).

In apocalyptic literature even the death of the righteous is not described as an end without hope, because meanwhile the belief in the awakening of the dead has gained ground (cf. Dan.12.1–3).

What had earlier been experienced as a severe temptation of faith has now become a symbol of salvation. Thus in the intertestamental period there evolved what amounted almost to a dogma of the suffering righteous, who will be raised up and shine in everlasting life. As already mentioned, this notion informed the songs of praise of the Qumranites, and it is most clearly expressed in the Wisdom of Solomon, especially in 2.12–20 and 5.1–7. This Book of Wisdom was written in Egypt, but the relevant passages probably stem from a Palestinian model, dating back to the first half of the first century B.C. It can therefore be assumed that Jesus and the early Church knew these texts. In Wisdom 2.12ff the enemies of the righteous speak, and if one did not know that this is a pre-Christian text, one would be inclined to think that the enemies of Jesus were saying: 'Let us lie in wait for the righteous man, because he is inconvenient to us and opposes our actions; he reproaches us for sins against the law. . . . He professes to have knowledge of God and calls himself a child of the Lord. . . . He calls the last end of the righteous happy, and boasts that God is his father. . . . Let us condemn him to a shameful death, for according to what he says he will be protected.' At the Last Judgement the righteous one confronts his enemies as a silent accuser, and the enemies profess their guilt: 'This is the man whom we once held in derision and made a byword of reproach—we fools! We thought that his life was madness and that his end was without honour.' (Wis. 5.4).

One may ask whether in the intertestamental era the figure of the suffering righteous man was not perhaps mingled with other figures. There exist indeed parallels between the prophet who dies because of his prophecy, the figure of the servant of the Lord in Isa.53 who dies as a redemption for the sins of others, and the martyrs who died for their testimony and whose sufferings have the power to redeem (cf. the Susanna legends and the second Book of Maccabees). Despite the influences which the various motifs exercised upon each other, there has been very little mingling of the different figures. The passages from the Book of Wisdom (2 and 5), quoted above, may well be a topical rendering of Isa.53, but the stress is not on the redeeming function of the servant of the Lord but on the sufferings of the prophet who, as such, was the archetype of the suffering righteous man (Isa.53.11).

iv *Jesus, the Crucified Righteous Man*

When the early Church discovered in Psalm 22 a key text to the understanding of Christ's crucifixion, much of what has been said above must also have come into play. It is, however, remarkable, that in the crucifixion narrative only the first words, as well as the beginning and the end of the description of the enemies (v. 1.7f and 18), are quoted, but not the expressions of trust nor the concluding song of praise.

Does this selective use of the text mean that the emphasis

should only be placed on the crucified one's god-forsakenness and on his being mocked by his enemies? The bitter memories of that must have been so vivid that there was no need to stress the repugnant details, but rather to unfold their meaning. Mark, who in this is probably following a pre-canonic tradition, does not quote the passages from the psalm as proof of the prophecy, using a formula such as: 'this was to fulfil the Scripture'. The point at issue in quoting Psalm 22 is not only to show formal congruity between specific verses of the psalm and specific details of the events at Golgotha, but to demonstrate a profound 'analogy of situation'. Not only the exact wording, but the meaning of the quoted passage from the Old Testament is important for the interpretation.

Jesus's cry is an allusion to the entire psalm, since in Old Testament and rabbinical usage the quotation of the first words of a book or a prayer indicated the entire book or prayer. It would in my view, however, be a mistake to make the universal and eschatological dimensions of the psalm's concluding verses so central to the interpretation of the cruci-fixion that the main accent is then placed on God's interven-tion and deliverance and on the ensuing song of praise. A tendency in this direction may be present in the manner of Matthew's later work of redaction on Mark's crucifixion narrative. But in Mark and in the pre-canonic crucifixion traditions the quotations from the psalm emphasize the *suffering* of the crucified who, in his death throes, turns to God and in prayer struggles through to the certainty of salvation.

Nowhere in the Old Testament or in intertestamental literature is the coming Messiah described as a suffering righteous man. But when the early Church pondered the scandalous event of the crucifixion, it recognized that, by inference from Psalm 22 and similar passages in the Scrip-tures and intertestamental literature, the crucified Messiah was *the* suffering righteous man. The crucifixion was thus a divine 'must'. All this the Messiah was *obliged* to suffer in order to enter into his glory. Only in this way could Jesus be the Messiah in the profoundest sense. Because he made God's cause wholly his own, he had to go the way to the cross.

There he was mocked by his enemies, abandoned by his friends, and even consigned to death by God himself. Yet even in the throes of death he does not turn to God, whose ways are incomprehensible, in desperate accusation, but like the supplicant of Psalm 22. He himself, or at least the early Church, recognized that God's cause will triumph as prophesied in the concluding verses of Psalm 22.

According to this very old tradition, the death of Jesus does not possess a soteriological meaning in the strict sense of the word. It is rather a christological interpretation of the crucifixion, and has at the same time the parenthetical function of consoling, that is to say of offering admonition *and* comfort: those who belong to the community of this Messiah, those who, in following Christ, make God's cause their own, share in the fate of the suffering righteous one, and are thus already on the way to the cross—and to glory.

2 Remembrance of Death: Judgement and Turning Point

The quotations from Psalm 22 are closely linked to the narrative tradition of the crucifixion. This has lately led again to the assumption that the pre-canonical account of the crucifixion had not only been formulated in the light of this psalm, but had its entire origin in it. There are, however, some basic facts, such as the death itself, the execution by crucifixion, and Golgotha as the place of execution, which cannot be derived from the psalm. Equally, important details such as the bearing of the cross by Simon of Cyrene, the *schema* of hours, the inscription on the cross, the darkness, the words about the temple and Elijah, the cry of death, and the rending of the temple curtains cannot be derived from Psalm 22. It is however to be assumed that details contained in the psalm were 'history-creating' as soon as the psalm had become a 'key text' for the interpretation of the crucifixion. But it would be wrong to maintain that the *entire* pre-canonical crucifixion narrative had its origins in the reflection on quotations of key-texts contained therein. In that case, why should there have been a crucifixion narrative at all? And what was the point of origin of this old account which later became such an important element of the four Gospels? Did the pre-canonical account already contain a distinctive theological direction and interpretation of the crucifixion?

i *The Search for the Earliest Account of the Crucifixion*

In the chapter about the event of the crucifixion I outlined which elements of the crucifixion narrative are based with certainty, or at least with probability, on solid historical memory (see pp. 23ff). We are now concerned with a different question: which details in these accounts go back to the earliest traditions? The earliest traditions may already have a marked theological slant and may contain more 'interpretations' than 'facts'. On the other hand, at the various stages of tradition up to the final redaction by the Evangelists, valuable recollections may nevertheless have been worked into the transmitted accounts. Research tends to mingle in a bewildering fashion the two different questions: What were the actual events? and What were the earliest traditions? However, if one wants to do justice to the process of the creation of tradition, these two questions cannot be entirely separated from each other, either. If, for instance, it is assumed that the inscription on the cross or Jesus's death cry are historical 'facts', then it is highly likely that the recollection of them was incorporated into the earliest tradition, even if these 'facts' could not be homogeneously built into the hypothetically earliest crucifixion narratives.

Most scholars assume that the passion story, and especially the account of the crucifixion contained therein, came into being as a continuous narrative at a very early stage. Some even think this happened at the time of the first generation of Christians. But as soon as one seeks to establish which scenes and verses belonged to this oldest narrative, one enters a maze of hypotheses. As a rule the Gospel of Mark is taken as the point of departure. The attempt is made, with the aid of form-critical methods, to trace the tradition from the final redaction back towards the earliest levels of traditions that were incorporated. The following tables set out the result of various studies in the original accounts of the crucifixion, carried out during the past fifty years.

Table A (p. 44) shows only those studies which are based on the assumption that the passages in Mark (15.20b–41) were developed from *one* original account of the crucifixion, with the addition of other traditions and modifications by redaction. If one compares the results assembled in that table, many of which are very persuasively argued, one is tempted to abandon altogether the search for the earliest account of the crucifixion. Indeed, the scholars listed in that table are unanimous only in regard to the place of crucifixion, the crucifixion itself, and Jesus's death cry. In all other respects opinions either differ widely or conflict. What one researcher sees as the earliest tradition, another considers to be a later addition or even a redaction by Mark. These divergences are partly, but not exclusively, caused by the mingling of the questions of what actually happened and what are the earliest traditions.

Matters are complicated further if one adds the results of another working hypothesis (cf Table B, p. 45). These studies assume not one original account of the crucifixion, which was amplified later, but several early traditions or even sources, which served the Evangelists in their work of redaction of the crucifixion narrative. There is little unanimity among the propounders of this hypothesis either.

It is outside the scope of this present study to take up a critical position with regard to any of these hypotheses, which have usually been propounded with impressive scholarliness and are based on decades of detailed exegetic research, nor am I competent to do so. The following remarks, therefore, do not claim to present to the reader a new, well-founded hypothesis regarding the question of the earliest crucifixion narrative. They are rather intended as preliminary thoughts, based on critical reading of the above studies, which lead to the following tentative working hypothesis:

(1) The search for one, or several, earliest crucifixion narratives has so far not yielded satisfactory results. The search should nevertheless not be abandoned as hopeless, for the following reasons. If it were possible to determine the earliest narrative passion tradition(s), this would give us very valuable insight into the life and thought of the early Church.

Secondly, only if one has gained some clarity as to the extent and nature of the transmitted traditions, can one make distinctions in the present Gospels between tradition and redaction, and thus examine the specific theological slant of the four Gospels.

(2) In my view, it must be assumed that the narrative crucifixion tradition did not begin with a single original account, which was modified, shortened, or amplified first by transmission and later by redaction. It is much more likely that already at the time when tradition was first formed, three different crucifixion traditions came into being: (a) One based on reflection on psalms of lament and praise (cf. sections 1(iii) and (iv)). This encapsulated recollected details of the event of the crucifixion, because they illustrated the deep 'analogy of situation' between the crucified one and the supplicants of the psalms. The crucified Messiah was here interpreted as the suffering and glorified righteous one. The nucleus of this first line of tradition is Jesus's recital of Psalm 22.1 and—in a variant of the same tradition—of Ps. 31.5. In the process of transmitting tradition, further details were added, which were derived from reflection on Scripture and not from the recollection of factual details. (b) An old eyewitness account of Simon of Cyrene, which was at first probably transmitted as a family tradition. Later perhaps other eyewitness accounts were amalgamated with it, such as those of the women and other onlookers present at Golgotha. (c) A further line of tradition with a strong theological bias was developed from the *schema* of hours and from the death cry of Jesus. It is probable that from the beginning, the account of three hours of darkness before Jesus's death also belonged to this tradition (see below, section 2(iii)).

(3) It is no longer possible to determine the exact extent and wording of these three lines of tradition. It is probable that the various communities of the early church transmitted differing versions of this oral tradition. Therefore the marked differences in the accounts of Mark and Matthew on the one hand, and Luke and John on the other, cannot solely be attributed to redaction by the Evangelists.

(4) It is also no longer possible to determine when, where, and how two or all three lines of tradition slowly merged or

THE EARLIEST TRADITIONS OF THE CRUCIFIXION

TABLE A

In the following table shaded areas indicate the passages which the respective scholars consider the earliest accounts of the crucifixion.

shaded areas = most probable
? = assumable

	Verse	Bultmann	Finegan	Grant	Taylor	Peddinghaus	Schweizer	Linnemann
Leading to crucifixion	20 b	▨		▨	▨	▨	▨	
Simon of Cyrene	21 a	▨	▨	▨	▨	▨	▨	
bears cross	b	▨		▨	▨	▨	▨	▨
Golgotha	22 a	▨		▨	▨	▨	▨	▨
Place of skull	b	▨		▨	▨	▨	▨	
Wine mingled with myrrh	23 a	▨		▨	▨	▨	▨	
Refusal	b	▨		▨	▨	▨	▨	
Crucifixion	24 a	▨	▨	▨	▨	▨	▨	
Division of garments	b		▨	▨	▨	▨	▨	
Third hour	25 a		?					▨
Crucifixion	b		▨	▨	▨	▨	▨	
Inscription	26 a			▨	▨	▨	▨	
King of Jews	b			▨	▨	▨	▨	
Two robbers	27 a	?		▨	▨	▨		
on his right and left	b			▨	▨	▨		
Mocking	29 a			▨	▨	▨	▨	
Wagging heads	b			▨	▨	▨	▨	
Temple	c			▨	▨	▨	▨	
Save yourself	30 a			▨	▨	▨	▨	
Come down	b			▨	▨	▨	▨	
Chief priests	31 a			▨	▨	▨	▨	
Cannot save himself	b			▨	▨	▨	▨	
Christ the King?	32 a			▨	▨	▨		
Those crucified with him	b			▨	▨	▨	?	▨
Sixth hour, darkness	33 a			▨	▨	▨	▨	▨
until ninth hour	b			▨	▨	▨	▨	▨
Ninth hour, cry	34 a			▨	▨	▨	▨	▨
Eloi, Eloi	b			▨	▨	▨	▨	▨
My God	c			▨	▨	▨	▨	
Bystanders	35 a			▨	▨	▨	▨	
Behold he is calling Elijah	b			▨	▨	▨	▨	
Sponge with vinegar	36 a			▨	▨	▨	?	
Wait, let us see	b			▨	▨	▨		
Cry	37 a	?	▨	▨	▨	▨	▨	▨
and death	b			▨	▨	▨	▨	▨
Rending of curtain	38 a			▨	▨	▨	▨	▨
top to bottom	b			▨	▨	▨		▨
Centurion	39 a			▨	▨	▨		
Truly, this man	b		▨					
Women looking on	40 a		▨					
Mary Magdalene, etc.	b							
From Galilee	41 a		▨					
Many others	b							

TABLE B

Knox explains duplications and divergences in the synoptic accounts of the crucifixion by claiming that the evangelists used independent sources which can still be recognized behind the following passages:

Disciple source: Mark 15.22–3, 24b–30, 33–9.
Twelve (?) source: Mark 15.21; Luke 23.32, 33b, 34a, 35a;
                        Mark 15.31–2; Luke 23.36–40, 42–3;
                        Mark 15.37; Luke 23.48.

Schreiber assumes that Mark combined two early crucifixion narratives by redaction, i.e. the following accounts:

1: Mark 15.20b–2a; 24; 27.
2: Mark 25.25, 26, 29a, 32c, 33, 34a, 37, 38.

Benoit and Boismard maintain in their synopsis of the four Gospels that, apart from the 'sayings' source, three other written documents (A, B, C) were used in the writing of the Gospels. Of these, document A (of Jewish-Christian origin) and document B (a revision of document A for the use of gentile Christian communities) were important for the crucifixion narrative and can still be recognized behind the following verses:

A: Matt. 27.33a; John 19.18a, 18b; (Matt. 27.37?); John 19.29; 30c; Luke 23.49.
B: (Mark 15.21?); Mark 15.22, 23, 24a, 24b, 26, 27, 31–32a, 33, 34a, 37b, 38, 39, 40–41.

were amalgamated by deliberate redaction. There again it is likely that various combinations and stages of development existed in the communities of the early Church. It is highly likely that the merging occurred at an early stage and almost certainly before Mark. It might be worth considering whether the second line of tradition, based on eyewitness accounts, was added to the crucifixion narrative at a relatively late stage, possibly by Mark himself. This would certainly be in line with a typical Marcan intention to stress in his Gospel that proper belief in the risen Lord means to conceive of him as mortal man who follows the way to the cross. The insertion of an old eyewitness account into the crucifixion narrative would thus not have been prompted by historical interest but by didactic intent.

ii Points of Origin in Worship

How did narrative crucifixion traditions come into being and why—by amalgamating these traditions—did pre-canonic crucifixion narratives come about? What is the point of origin of the creation and transmission of tradition?

It has sometimes been contended that there existed inter-testamental and later rabbinical and Christian legends of martyrs, and it was assumed that the early Church, with the crucifixion narrative, had created a similar legend of the martyrdom of Christ. This may be partly accurate as far as later redactions are concerned (cf. chapter 4, 4 below, regarding the Lucan narrative). As far as the pre-canonic narrative is concerned, this assumption is improbable. Firstly, stories of martyrs presuppose biographical interest, which obviously did not exist in the early Church. Secondly, the martyr's death was frequently combined with concepts of the redeeming power of death, which in the earliest crucifixion narratives is either lacking or of secondary importance only.

It is maintained more frequently that the pre-canonic passion narrative came into being with apologia and missionary sermons in mind. As a consequence, the narrative is considered to be an amplification of the early Church's 'confessions' and hymns, and especially of the statement contained in 1 Cor. 15.3b. But the purpose of this statement was hardly that of a missionary sermon. If 1 Cor. 15.3b had influenced the narrative, it would be difficult to explain why the earliest narrative crucifixion traditions do not stress the central statement that '(Christ) died for our sins'; equally, they lack the apologetic tendency to invoke Scripture as proof.

More probable, in my view, than the two propositions above, is the assumption that the passion narrative was assembled for the purpose of worship and, in the early Church, was transmitted mainly by way of divine service. One hypothesis worth considering maintains that the passion narrative came into being as an anamnesis, that is to say as a recalling of the night of betrayal (from the last supper to

Peter's denial), the events of the crucifixion, and the 'occurrences' at the tomb. Remembrance of the night of betrayal was an established rite of the early Church. With a view to such a 'liturgical nightwatch', the self-contained account of the night of betrayal might have come into being and have been transmitted by narrating these recollections. The account of the crucifixion, structured in three parts by means of the *schema* of hours, might indicate narrative recollection of the events of the crucifixion during the three hours of prayer ordained by Jewish-Christian ritual. Such remembrance, at first, probably took place each Friday, and later only once a year, on Good Friday. The accounts of the events at the tomb may have been assembled with a view to the earliest celebrations of Easter at Christ's tomb, and transmitted during these celebrations. We know too little about the services of the early Church to be able to voice anything more definite than assumptions regarding the *Sitz im Leben* (or, more specifically, the liturgical function) of the pre-canonic passion story.

Studies of the history of liturgy point to the assumption that remembrance of Jesus's death and resurrection characterized the services of the early Church. It is therefore probable that in earlier times, in the celebration of the Eucharist, anamnesis was more extensive than is the case today. Not only was Christ's redeeming death invoked, but his passion was remembered and recounted. It is impossible, though, to trace this history of liturgy in all details back to the early Church, and it is likely that even then there existed differing liturgical practices. It is worth noting, however, that a number of scholars, often from quite different points of departure, and by way of conflicting arguments, have come to assume that the pre-canonic passion narrative had its origin in divine service. They have, for instance, pointed to parallels in the Jewish service, which also contains anamnesis of God's acts of salvation, such as the Exodus. Among the Qumranites the songs of thanksgiving to the Teacher of Justice played a similar role. It has also been deduced from the narrative style of Mark 15 that it had its origin in divine service, since the repetitions contained in the crucifixion narrative are indicative of anamnesis. To extend the search for the exact origins of the crucifixion narrative beyond the above assumptions is an interesting but excessively hypothetical undertaking. Is the point of origin to be looked for in the Greek wing of the community at Jerusalem, which was influenced by Stephen, in the Jewish Christian community of Bethany, in the diaspora community of Antioch, or elsewhere? All these propositions have been put forward in recent years. But if the crucifixion narrative did indeed originate as liturgical remembrance of Christ's death, as described above, this may have happened simultaneously in the various communities of the early Church.

iii *Crucifixion: Judgement and Turning Point*

Did the earliest account of the crucifixion already contain a distinct theological direction? According to the working hypothesis proposed in section 2 (i), this account is a combination of three different lines of tradition. It is therefore to be assumed that it embodies not one, but several, theological interpretations. One of these has already been discussed in section 1 (iv), i.e. the christological interpretation of the crucifixion which stresses the necessity of suffering, and recognizes the Messiah in the suffering righteous man. The second line of tradition, based on the family tradition of the eyewitness Simon of Cyrene, testifies to the historical fact of the crucifixion without giving it any specific theological meaning. But the mere fact that the memory of this repugnant event was not repressed, indicates that the early Church considered it as theologically significant.

The third line of tradition mentioned above gained particular importance for theological interpretation. It briefly narrates the crucifixion at the third hour, but the main stress is placed on the darkness from the sixth until the ninth hour, when darkness ended. It is likely that, from the beginning, or at least from a very early stage, the account of the rending of the temple curtain also belonged to this line of tradition, which was probably incorporated very early into the pre-canonic crucifixion narrative.

It has frequently been said that this tradition gives an apocalyptic interpretation of Jesus's death. Many texts from the Old Testament and from intertestamental books, as well as statements contained in the New Testament and in non-biblical apocalyptic literature, are cited in support. Indeed, the prophetic-apocalyptic literature of the Old Testament describes the judgement day as darkness (Amos 8.9; Isa. 13.10; Joel 2.1ff, 10ff; 3.14ff; Zeph. 1.15). There are also prophecies that the voice of God will be heard on the day of judgement (Amos 1.2; Jer. 25.30ff; Ps. 46.6). There are further prophecies regarding the coming destruction of the temple (Mic. 3.12; Jer. 7.13ff; 24.4–6). But neither the Old Testament nor intertestamental texts connect these three signs of judgement with each other. In addition, the signs associated with the crucifixion have other meanings, unconnected with judgement. The darkness can, for instance, be associated with the myth of the dark cosmic waters in the stories of Genesis and in Exodus. If this latter were the main association contained in the tradition on which Mark 15.33 was based, then Jesus's death would not first and foremost mean judgement, but a new genesis and a new exodus. The significance of the rending of the temple curtain has been disputed in the exegesis of the church Fathers as well as in modern commentaries. If its meaning is taken to be the curtain that separates the holy from the holiest of holies in the temple, then the sign must indicate that the holiest of holies is now there for all to see, because through Christ's death the insurmountable barrier between man and God has become surmountable and the gate to heaven has been opened. If the richly adorned curtain that separates the holy and the temple's entrance hall is meant, then the sign would mean the end to the exclusion of non-priests and non-Jews from the place where God is present, and thus indicate the end of Jewish temple services altogether. One can also understand the rending of the (inner or outer) curtain as symbolic for the threatened or actual destruction of the temple itself. There are indications for each of these interpretations in biblical and non-biblical literature.

One should, however, not draw too far-reaching conclusions from such ambiguous symbols. The pointer to frequently rather disparate 'parallels' between biblical and non-biblical literature can lead to interpretations which cease to have much to do with the signs so briefly and soberly described in Mark 15. It is to be assumed, though, that these signs are mentioned for theological reasons and are not intended to report historical facts. What theological interpretation of Christ's death is thus presented?

The style of this third narrative crucifixion tradition is prophetic-apocalyptic. Prophetic-apocalyptic literature either relates events which are to come or judges present events in the light of God's future actions. But in this crucifixion tradition events which have already come to pass are related in prophetic-apocalyptic language. It is a bold interpretation of Christ's death: the seemingly insignificant events at Golgotha have in reality a universal, or rather an eternal importance. With Jesus's death, darkness did not fall upon the whole earth; on the contrary, darkness was at an end. What happened on the cross was anticipated last judgement and thus a turning point, a new beginning.

But here, too, the statement '(he) died for our sins', which plays such an important part in the creed of the early Church, is absent. The soteriological significance of Jesus's death in this narrative tradition is not proclaimed by indicating the redeeming nature of Jesus's dying for the sins of others. The point here is rather the unfolding of the cosmic and theological meaning of the events at Golgotha. Because Christ's death has anticipated the last judgement and has created a new beginning, the early Church, in its remembrance of his death, was able to celebrate joyfully the turning point that happened with it. This, in turn, led to belief in the soteriological effect of his death, as expressed in the formulae and hymns of the early Church which will be discussed below.

3   The Belief in Christ's Death: He Died for Us

The interpretations we have discussed so far gave the precanonic crucifixion narrative its theological character. But apart from those narrative traditions, there existed in the early Church other thoughts regarding the significance of Jesus's death. This is reflected in particular in credal formulae and hymns. We meet with these in quotations and allusions in Paul's Epistles, as well as in fragments of formulae and songs contained in other passages of the New Testament.

i *Credal Formulae and Songs*

It is not easy to determine what genuinely belongs to pre-canonic credal formulae. The main text (1 Cor. 15.3ff), which is the subject of section (iii), is heralded expressly as pre-Pauline tradition. The other texts cited below are also usually regarded as being pre-canonic credal formulae and songs.

Was there to begin with a shorter or longer 'original' creed which was amplified in transmission and adapted to meet differing purposes? Some scholars hold this opinion. They think, for instance, that in the beginning the creed was, 'Jesus is the Christ/Messiah', or '*Christos Kyrios*' (Christ is the Lord/Ruler). Thereafter, this original creed was amplified with elements from the second article of the present creed, and in the encounter with the non-Jewish world, elements from the first and third articles were added. To meet different circumstances and different purposes, the 'original creed' was thus further developed.

In my view, it is more probable that from the beginning several credal formulae and songs were developed. Even before the existence of such Christian formulae, the Jewish Christians were able to join in with the confessional *schema* (Deut. 6.4–7) of 'the Lord our God is one Lord' which was recited twice daily. This main message of the Jewish mission in a polytheistic Hellenic civilization thus also became an important element of the Christian creed.

Much more central, however, are the statements about Jesus. They can be put into several categories. It is for instance remarkable that in the formulae of belief and annunciation, the title 'Christ' is usually combined with 'Jesus, who died for us' and was raised by God. The title '*kyrios*' on the other hand, appears in formulae of worship, in which the congregation confesses its belief that the Lord is present during service and places itself under his rule 'now'. An Aramaic form of the title '*kyrios*' appears also in connection with the celebration of the Lord's Supper as '*maranatha*', which can be translated as 'our Lord, come!' The title 'Son of God' indicates the one whom God adopted and exalted; this appears in formulae which speak of the pre-existent one who was sent into the world 'for us' and was sacrificed. The differing religious and cultural environments of the early communities led, from the beginning, to varying acclamations, creeds and confessional songs.

According to a study of this subject, the original Aramaic-speaking community mainly employed formulae of awakening and the *maranatha*-call. The Hellenistic semitic and gentile Christian communities developed catechetic formulae about salvation (for instance, formulae of God giving his Son and of death), and about the person of Jesus (for instance, the baptismal creed, stating the belief in the Son of God, and later amplifications of it, taking in also central events of Jesus's life). Invocations and hymns used in worship also originated with the Hellenistic gentile Christian communities.

If one examines the statements these credal formulae and songs contain about the significance of Jesus's crucifixion, one can observe the following:

(1) Only about half of all early Christian formulae speak expressly of Jesus's suffering and death. It was possible to confess one's belief in Jesus without mentioning his death on the cross, as for instance in the song of confession quoted in 1 Tim. 3.16.

(2) Details from the pre-canonical crucifixion narrative appear only in the post-canonical confessions contained in the letters of Ignatius, and there only summarily. Also, in the formulae which expressly mention Jesus's passion and death, one cannot detect a uniform terminology, nor a uniform interpretation of his death. In the formulae of resurrection, the fact of Jesus's death is presupposed, without expressly mentioning or interpreting it (for instance, Rom. 10.9; 1 Cor. 6.14; 1 Thess. 1.10). In the song of Phil. 2.6–11, death is only a transitory stage on Jesus's path, a proof of his obedience. In the formulae of God giving his Son and of death (for instance, Rom. 8.31ff; Gal. 1.4; Eph. 5.2; Rom. 5.6; 1 Cor. 8.11; 1 Thess. 5.10), the resurrection of Jesus is often not mentioned, but his death is usually interpreted as one of vicarious redemption.

(3) These formulae could be used differently in different situations and thus their theological direction also changed. For instance, in 1 Pet. 2.21ff the formula of death is used in a

quite novel way. Originally the emphasis had been entirely on vicarious atonement. By amplification from Isa. 53, this formula was then modified to enjoin ethical conduct on the community, and Christ's redeeming death was turned essentially into an example.

ii *Isaiah 53 and Christ's Redeeming Death*

The part played by reflection on Scripture in interpreting Jesus's death is under dispute. We shall therefore only examine the influence of the most frequently discussed text from Scripture—Isaiah 53. Indeed, in the theological debate about the soteriological meaning of Christ's death no text from the Old Testament is cited as often as the song of the suffering servant of the Lord in Isa. 52.13—53.12. It comes always as a surprise, therefore, that this 'proto-gospel of the passion', or whatever we like to call this fourth servant's song, is quoted relatively rarely in the New Testament—specifically only seven times in all.

The many scholars who have time and again considered the question of the influence of Isa. 53 on the statements about Christ's redemptive death in the New Testament, have so far not reached unanimous conclusions. Some maintain that, despite the small number of quotations, this text from the Old Testament strongly influenced the early Church's theological reflections on the meaning of Jesus's death, and that this was already the case in the Aramaic-speaking semitic Christian communities. Others reject this claim completely and maintain that Isa. 53 influenced the concept of the redemptive death only in very few passages, that in the thinking of the early Church it gained ground very slowly and began to play an important role only later on.

In order to form one's own opinion in this dispute, it is advisable first to consider the difficult Isaiah text itself and then to examine the quotations from and allusions to the servant's song as they appear in the New Testament. In this one immediately encounters a first, much discussed, hurdle: the Greek translation of Isa. 53 (LXX) deviates markedly from the Hebrew original (HT)! It is also possible that in some instances neither of these versions served as a model, but that an old targum was used, i.e. a free Aramaic translation. The list of quotations and allusions from a proponent of the first school of thought mentioned above, would look as follows (express quotations in italics):

Isa. 52.13 (LXX)	My servant shall prosper	Acts 3.13; 2.31, 33 John 12.23–32 etc.; Phil. 2.9
Isa. 52.15 (LXX)	They shall see	*Rom. 15.21*
Isa. 53.1 (LXX)	Who has believed?	*Rom. 10.16; John 12.38*
Isa. 53.3 (HT?)	A man of sorrows. . . . despised	Mark 9.12
Isa. 53.4 (HT?)	carried our sorrows	*Matt. 8.17*
Isa. 53.5 (HT?)	with his stripes we were healed	*1 Pet. 2.24*
Isa. 53.6 (LXX?)	we like sheep have gone astray	*1 Pet. 2.25*
Isa. 53.7–8a LXX)	like a lamb	*Acts 8.32–3*
Isa. 53.9 (LXX?)	no violence, no deceit	*1 Pet. 2.22*
Isa. 53.10 (HT)	an offering for sin	Rom. 8.3
Isa. 53.11 (LXX?)	bear their iniquities	*1 Pet. 2.24*
Isa. 53.11–12 (HT?)	the sin of many	Mark 10.45; 14.24
Isa. 53.12 (HT?)	divide him a portion with the great	Luke 11.21–2
Isa. 53.12 (LXX)	numbered with the transgressors	*Luke 22.37*
Isa. 53.12 (LXX)	poured out . . .	Rom. 4.25
Isa. 53.12 (HT)	poured out his soul to death	Phil. 2.7–8
Isa. 53.12 (LXX)	bore the sin of many	Heb. 9.28
Isa. 53.12 (HT?)	made intercession	Rom. 8.34

One might consider whether other texts in the New Testament are influenced by Isa. 53, such as 1 Cor. 11.23–5; 15.3, as well as general formulae of God giving his Son and those containing the statement 'for us' or 'for our sins', mentioned in section 3 (i). Furthermore, 1 Tim. 2.6; 1 Pet. 3.18; and many passages from John, for instance John 1.29; 10.11, 15, 17, 18; 1 John 2.1, 29; 3.7; 2.2; 4.10; 3.5; and the twenty-eight passages about the lamb in Revelation.

How did the Christians of the early Church read the song of the servant of the Lord? Is there, as in the case of Ps. 22, a history of interpretation of the Old Testament and inter-testamental literature which influenced the early Christian understanding of it? In answering this question, the proponents of the two opposing theories are unanimous: in the late texts of the Old Testament and in the intertestamental period, Isa. 53 played almost no part at all. The text is never quoted, and where its influence is recognizable, either the point is to stress the supremacy of the Lord, or the suffering servant of God is conceived as the suffering righteous or martyr (but the concept of the vicarious redeeming death is not present).

What gives the passage its decisive character, i.e. the suffering to redeem the many (=all) that leads to glory, is never mentioned. Nor is there any evidence from the pre-Christian era of the expectation of a Messiah who will suffer for the sake of all others. If the early Christians, in their interpretation of Christ's death as one of vicarious redemption, did indeed go back to Isa. 53, they could not have derived this concept from the Old Testament or from intertestamental sources. Thus they would have given quite a new interpretation to the servant's song and to the concept of the Messiah, which in their time and to their contemporaries would have been both startling and objectionable.

Many scholars maintain that this is what did happen. They point out that, according to the list above, almost all verses of the fourth servant's song are either quoted or alluded to in the main texts of the New Testament, and that therefore the entire song, and not only individual statements from it, belonged to the 'Bible of the early Church'. According to them, this text had from the beginning strongly influenced theological thought and had led to the belief that Jesus is the suffering servant of the Lord. Many contend that Jesus saw himself as the suffering servant and had revealed this also to his disciples. This creed is given varying emphases in the New Testament. A study of the subject has distinguished four traditions of interpretation: from the explanatory words about the wine at the last supper was developed a eucharistic-soteriological tradition ('died for our sins'); parallel to this, the early Church had developed a tradition of healing ('through his wounds we have been healed'); the christological tradition of interpretation had its origin in the prophecies of suffering and in Acts 8.32ff (the suffering

Messiah); and from Mark 10.45 had been developed the tradition of Jesus as the example, also strongly evident in 1 Pet. 2.21ff. Despite these different traditions of interpretation, the proponents of the view mentioned above maintain that, from the beginning, the central statement contained in the servant's song, i.e. the triumph of the sufferer who redeems the sins of others, had been the main point of all quotations and allusions to Isa. 53 in the New Testament. In this connection it is, for instance, pointed out that the words of the Communion and the formulae of 'God giving his Son' and of vicarious redemption, which are all influenced by Isa. 53, form part of the most ancient creed of the early Church.

A second group of scholars take a different view: that, considering the atomistic use of Scripture at that period, it would not be justifiable to take all allusions to the servant's song equally into account. Only those quotations and allusions which expressly state the redeeming death for the sins of others are to be considered relevant in trying to determine the origin of interpreting Christ's death as one of vicarious redemption. If one examines the above table of quotations and allusions in the light of this criterion, it is narrowed down considerably. The only quotation contained in the passion narratives (Luke 22.37) does not point to redemption. Of the six remaining quotations only 1 Pet. 2.21–5 speaks of the redeeming death (not in order to proclaim this concept, but to teach Jesus as an example of Christian patience). Acts 8.32–5 speaks of Jesus's willingness to die and of his humiliation, but not of his redeeming the sins of others. Many of the other allusions must also be excluded unless one accepts that the formulae of God giving his Son and the statements 'for us' or 'for our sins' should be traced back to Isa. 53. And of all the passages that allude to 'poured out his soul' only two remain, i.e. Rom. 4.25 and Mark 10.45. The second group of scholars, therefore, do not—or only in rare instances—trace back to Isa. 53 the interpretation of Christ's death as one of redemption. In their opinion, the early Church derived the concept of vicarious redemption from Palestinian and Greek Judaism of the period and, according to them, this interpretation was only later associated with the Isa. 53 testimony from Scripture. In this dispute it is impossible to form anything but tentative views, since so little is known about the beginnings of theological thought in the early Church. It is, in my opinion, probable that the interpretation of Christ's death as one of vicarious redemption came about in the following manner:

In the beginning was the repugnant death on the cross. Through meditating on the songs of lament and praise in the Scriptures, the early Church recognized the divine 'must' of the passion. In its services it recalled the passion of the crucified and risen Messiah and looked forward to his return. In doing so, the early Church also learnt to conceive of the crucifixion as an eschatological and cosmic event. Yet the repugnance of the crucifixion was not to be eradicated. Why had God delivered the Messiah into the hands of his enemies? What had been the meaning of this divine 'must'?

The urgency of these questions and the possibility of discovering the startling answer to them can only be understood if one bears in mind the Old Testament statements about sacrifice. On the one hand, believers, whose thinking had been formed by the Old Testament, knew of the redeeming power of sacrifice. At the time of Jesus, daily sacrifices were made in the temple at Jerusalem and the feast of the Atonement was celebrated every year. On the other hand, the notion of human sacrifice was something horrendous to Old Testament believers. The prophets of Jehovah had condemned the human sacrifices to Moloch as abominable idolatry. Jehovah himself had demanded from Abraham the willingness to sacrifice, but had prevented the sacrifice of Isaac. How, in these circumstances, could Jesus's death be understood as an atoning sacrifice?

The fourth servant's song probably played a threefold role in this:

(1) The memory of Jesus was still powerful. Whether Jesus had seen himself as the suffering servant of the Lord and had taught his disciples accordingly, can no longer be determined. But there did exist a profound analogy of passion and triumph between Jesus and the servant of the Lord. The memory of this must lead the early Church sooner or later to a christological interpretation of Isa. 53 and to understand Christ's death as one of vicarious redemption.

(2) Based on Old Testament notions of atonement by sacrifice, and on contemporary statements about the redeeming power of the suffering of the righteous, the early Church began to recognize in the first decade after Jesus's death that Christ had 'died for us', 'for our sins'. This may have happened simultaneously in the Aramaic and Greek Jewish-Christian communities. Since, at the same time, the early Church searched the Old Testament for key texts in order to comprehend the crucifixion, it soon discovered the tremendous statement contained in Isa. 53, which had not been understood for many centuries.

(3) This could happen all the more easily and quickly as the same passage from Isaiah had already been associated in intertestamental literature with the psalms about the suffering righteous. The Jehovah-word of Isa. 52.13–15 puts the middle section (Isa. 53.1–11a) into the mouths of peoples and kings, as a confession of guilt in the form of a song of thanksgiving. Therefore, the very structure of Isa. 53 led to the perception that the Messiah was not only the suffering and delivered righteous one, but also the servant of the Lord who suffers and triumphs for our sake.

iii   1 Cor. 15.3—5: The Earliest Article of Faith?

There is no doubt that the most important formulation of faith which has come down to us from Paul is contained in 1 Cor. 15.3–5. It is not intended here to marshal the many questions that present-day discussions of this text have produced, or to adopt a point of view. Questions regarding the relations between the Twelve, between the Apostles and Paul, or the lately much-discussed significance of the 'three days', fall outside the scope of this book. We shall only examine that which is connected with the sentence—stemming from early Christian tradition—'Christ died for our sins.' It is a very ancient statement of faith, and Paul solemnly introduces it, using an established formula for the transmission of an article of faith (vv. 1–3a). The literal translation of the text is as follows:

(3b)   'that Christ died   for our sins
                                  in accordance with the scriptures

	(4a) and that he was buried
(4b) and that he was raised	on the third day
	in accordance with the scriptures
	(5a) and that he appeared
	(5b) to Cephas, then to the twelve.'

By giving this translation and presenting it in the above manner, an attitude has already been adopted in regard to three questions under dispute:

(1) The formula comprises verses 3b–5. Some scholars, however, are of the opinion that v. 5b does not properly belong to it, while others include v. 7, and some even the entire statement of vv. 6–7.

(2) The formula is a homogeneous piece of tradition. However, some scholars assume that Paul did no more than combine several credal formulae by linking one of death, one of burying, and one of raising by 'and that', and adding in v. 5 and 7 two further legitimizing formulae.

(3) The credal formula consists of two main statements with three explanatory additions to each. From the style of the text, the formula might also be considered to have a four-part structure (vv. 3b; 4a; 4b; 5), or a three-part structure (vv. 3b; 4; 5).

It is equally difficult to form a view concerning another much disputed question: was the original text of 1 Cor. 15.3–5 in Greek or in Hebrew/Aramaic? There is no doubt that the formula contains not only 'non-Pauline' concepts and turns of phrase, but also semitic expressions. Typical for semitic languages are, for instance, the parallelism of individual statements, the monotonous 'and that', the passive form of the verb, 'was raised' (which indirectly implies God), and the Aramaic form of the name of 'Cephas' instead of 'Simon' (as in the parallel passage, Luke 24.34). It has further been assumed that the version of Isa. 53, on which 1 Cor. 15.3 might possibly have been based, was not the Greek translation of the Old Testament, but the Isaiah targum. But it might equally be argued that the Greek-speaking Jewish Christians were strongly influenced by the Septuagint and its 'semitisms', and that any direct influence of Isa. 53 is uncertain. Neither the arguments for or against a Hebrew/Aramaic original are really convincing, and the question as to the idiom of the original text can no longer be decided. But we may assume that Palestinian material was worked into this statement of faith. We have here a creed that stems from the middle thirties or early forties of the first century. Paul may have come to know the formula shortly after his call to Damascus, or later in Jerusalem, possibly even later still in Antioch. He did not use this traditional material slavishly, but translated and cited it freely, for apart from semitic turns of phrase it contains many recognizably Pauline expressions.

Despite the great age of 1 Cor. 15.3b–5, it is probably not the earliest creed. While the formulae discussed in section 3 (i) only stress either the dying or the rising from the dead, we have here one that emphasizes both aspects equally. The remark 'according to the scriptures' which is missing in other formulae, is here repeated twice for greater emphasis. The formula has also been amplified by 'proofs' of the actual death ('buried' v. 4a) and the actual resurrection ('appeared' v. 5). The tradition, which Paul passed on, was originally probably shorter and underwent various stages of development before it reached him.

The putative history of this tradition can be seen in two ways: either a formula of death and another of resurrection were combined at a very early stage and were amplified later, or 1 Cor. 15.3b–5 was developed from a shorter version, such as the one behind 2 Cor. 5.15. But if one considers that Paul must already have known this tradition in the form in which he transmitted it, either towards the end of the thirties or in the early forties, there was little time for a history of tradition to develop. It can therefore not be excluded that this formula was developed in its present form either in Jerusalem or in another Jewish Christian community, possibly with a view to catechesis.

After considering the above remarks regarding the structure, language, form, and function of 1 Cor. 15.3b–5, we are now concerned with the much more important question: what bearing has this ancient tradition on the interpretation of Christ's death, especially if compared with the interpretations discussed earlier, on pp. 38ff and pp. 48ff? The following statements seem of importance to me:

'Christ died': The accent does not lie, as in the earliest crucifixion narrative and also in later Pauline writings, on the manner of his death, namely on the cross. The repugnant event of the crucifixion is no more emphasized here than in other credal formulae. It is however pointed out that *Christ* died. The pagan Christian community of Corinth probably just took it to be his name, but for the semitic Christian community it was of extreme significance that Jesus died as Christ/Messiah. The first statement of 1 Cor. 15.3b runs parallel to the christological interpretation of Jesus's death obtained from Ps. 22. The events of the passion reshaped the concept of the Messiah held by pious Jews who had become Christians. The Messiah, as the righteous one, had to suffer and to die. While other verbs of this formula take the passive form, 'died' is the active form. Perhaps this may be taken to imply that Jesus, as Christ, went deliberately to his death.

'For our sins': With this statement the formula turns into a line of interpretation which in the earliest crucifixion narrative is alluded to only vaguely, if at all. Although the 'must' of the death is also taken for granted here, it is now not interpreted as a cosmic judgement and turning point of history, but as vicarious redemption. Thus 1 Cor. 15.3b–5 is in the same line of tradition as most of the formulae of God giving his Son and of death cited in section 3 (i). The Greek preposition *hyper*, which is used in all these formulae, as well as in the preface of the Communion service, can be translated variously as 'in favour of', 'instead of', 'in view of', 'for'. Depending on the formula, all these meanings can be implied. First of all, Jesus died for our sins. In the 'for us/you' there is also an implication of 'instead of us', but in the much rarer and more specific expression 'for our sins' the accent is placed differently. Here the vicarious sacrifice is emphasized clearly and *hyper* can best be translated as 'for the redemption/eradication of sins'.

'In accordance with the scriptures': Does this general reference to Scriptures refer only to 'died' or to 'for our sins'? From a purely grammatical point of view, either is possible. The second, identical reference to Scriptures in v. 4b does not help to elucidate this point, since it can equally refer to 'raised' as to 'on the third day'. The question must therefore

be decided by the specific theological direction of the formula. In its meditations on Scripture, and on the psalms of lament and praise in particular, the early Church had come to recognize that the Messiah had to die and to be raised. The reference to Scriptures can therefore be taken to refer to the verbs and thus mainly to those passages in the Old Testament and intertestamental literature cited in sections 1 (iii) and (iv). But the main accent of the first part of the formula lies in the interpretation of Christ's death as one of vicarious redemption. It is furthermore quite possible that the parallel statement in the second part of the formula ('on the third day') is not intended as the communication of a historical fact, but as a theological interpretation of the resurrection. Therefore the references to Scriptures probably point to the words immediately preceding them. Does this mean that there is an echo of Isa. 53 in 1 Cor. 15.3b or that the targum is quoted and translated? After what has been said in section 3 (ii), the first alternative is a possibility, the second seems improbable. The reference to Scriptures is general, and is not aimed at an individual passage but at the entire complex of concepts contained in the 'Bible of the early Church'. Therefore, Isa. 53 will also have to be borne in mind in this connection, but not exclusively. The invocation of Scriptures also includes Old Testament concepts of sacrifice and intertestamental concepts of the redeeming death of the suffering and then triumphant righteous.

'*And that* . . .': In contrast to the cosmic-theological interpretation discussed in section 2(iii), according to which, in Jesus's passion and death, judgement and eternal turning point are accomplished, 1 Cor. 15.3b–5 shows the redeeming death of Christ as one act in the context of the story of salvation. The burying is expressly mentioned, and according to Jewish concepts that would mean the absolute end of life. Thus the raising from the dead is not depicted as the expected salvation and glorification the righteous can hope for, but as another act, next to the death. In addition, the verbal form employed in the Greek text emphasizes something that cannot be rendered in translation: the formulae of resurrection usually use the verb in the aorist, which indicates a simple past event. In 1 Cor. 15.3b–5 all verbs are in the aorist, but there is one exception. The 'raised' in v. 4b is in the perfect, which often denotes the ongoing effect of a past event. This may be taken to imply that the raised Jesus is now present. With Christ's death of redemption the story of salvation has not ended, but just begun.

3

The Word of the Cross:
Pauline Interpretations

Paul, the Pharisee, was schooled in scriptural study and practised it assiduously both before and after his fateful encounter with the risen Lord. Even before his conversion on the way to Damascus, in his disputes with Christians, he had become acquainted with the 'Bible of the early Church' and its exegesis of Christ and the Kingdom to come. After his conversion, Paul continued his reflection on Scripture and derived his new interpretation of Christ's death from it.

Paul, the persecutor of Christians, witnessed the Martyrdom of Stephen. Although the account of the first martyrdom in Acts 7 probably contains more Lucan theology than historical memory, the event served to remind those who persecuted the Christians that Jesus had been crucified. After his conversion, Paul took part in the services of the early Church and thereby learnt to remember Christ's death and to expect his return.

Paul, 'zealous for the traditions of his fathers' (Gal. 1.14), must certainly have heard some of the early Church's credal formulae even before his conversion. After his baptism, he learnt and taught these traditions fervently, yet without slavishness. But he had become the servant of Christ (Rom. 1.1) and had thereby gained the freedom in every new situation to conserve, preach, and interpret anew the gospel he had received.

All three traditions of interpreting the crucifixion, discussed in the previous chapter, were known to Paul. How did he in turn pass them on to the 'young Churches' that were founded within a Hellenistic civilization? What new insight about the meaning of the crucifixion did he gain from his missionary disputes?

In this chapter we cannot be concerned with the examination of Paul's relationship with the Scriptures and with tradition, nor with his attitudes in diverse missionary situations. There exist several publications which give a summary of Paul's interpretation of the crucifixion and it is for this reason unnecessary to repeat it here. In what follows, therefore, we shall only examine, with the aid of two case studies, how Paul preached the gospel of the crucified Christ in two concrete situations: (1) in his disputes with the Christians of Corinth, and (2) in the critical situation of the communities of Galatia.

1 For the Corinthians: The Cross as Criterion

The apostle Paul came to Corinth about twenty years after the crucifixion had taken place. For some eighteen months, probably from the winter of A.D. 50 until the summer of A.D. 52, he conducted his missionary work in Achaia from there. This sojourn was the beginning of the apostle's often tense relations with the community at Corinth, as is made clear by his Epistles to them.

i Paul at Corinth

According to his own account, Paul began his missionary work 'in weakness and in much fear and trembling' (1 Cor. 2.3). Whether this was because of the preceding events in Macedonia and Athens (Acts 16—17), because of illness, or due to the evil reputation of the port of Corinth, can no longer be determined. From a purely human point of view, the atmosphere of Corinth must have been far from promising.

Situated between two ports, the old Corinth had developed into the capital of Greece and become a powerful centre of trade. This was viewed with displeasure by Roman merchants, and in response to a Greek challenge in 146 B.C. the Roman legions captured, sacked, and destroyed the old town. Some hundred years later, Caesar founded the new Corinth, at first as a colony for Roman veterans and freed slaves. Thanks to its favourable geographic situation and its position as provincial capital of southern and central Greece, the new

Corinth also developed into a large and prosperous trading port. In this way the originally purely Italic settlement gained a Hellenistic character, since, attracted by trade, Greeks came to settle and soon there also arrived large numbers of foreign settlers—an extensive Jewish colony, Egyptians, and other orientals—who all brought their own forms of worship with them. The earlier plan to open up the isthmus by a canal and thereby to increase trade even further, was reconsidered and held to be feasible, but then suddenly abandoned. The famous Isthmian Games again took place at Corinth, but were now 'enriched' by Roman gladiatorial contests. Like every port, the new Corinth was a place of vice, a reputation the earlier city had also shared. But not all that has been said about the vices of old Corinth should be automatically imputed to the new Corinth—in particular the frequently-quoted statement that there 'were well over a thousand prostitutes in the temple of Aphrodite'. This is based on an account of the old Corinth by Strabo, and was most likely an exaggeration even then. In the new town there existed only a small temple to Aphrodite on the Acrocorinth.

In this polyglot society, shaped by the pursuit of riches and pleasures, Paul preached his message of the crucified Christ. The somewhat fragmentary account of it in Acts 18 is probably accurate, since it fits well into the picture of events we gain from the Epistles to the Corinthians. As was his custom, Paul taught first at the synagogue and earned his living as a tentmaker in the house of the Christian Jews, Aquila and Priscilla, who had been banished from Rome. When his fellow workers, Silas and Timothy, came to Corinth from Macedonia, Paul was probably able to devote his entire time to his missionary work. Only a few Jews —among them the ruler of the synagogue, Crispus— accepted the gospel. But among the worshippers of God the message found greater response, and the centre of Paul's activities was transferred to the house next to the synagogue, belonging to the worshipper of God, Titus Justus. The scene at the tribunal before the proconsul Gallio, so dramatically described in Acts 18.12ff, probably brought Paul's fruitful sojourn at Corinth to an end. This, however, did not mean an end to the thanksgiving, care, and guidance Paul extended to the community he had 'created' with his message of the gospel (1 Cor. 4.15).

Unfortunately, we do not know exactly how Paul guided his young community through its 'birth pangs' and first steps. His Epistles all stem from the second phase of his missionary work, and the sermons in Acts show a more Lucan than Pauline vision of this mission. Based on the first Epistle to the Corinthians, the following can at any rate be said:

At the start of Paul's missionary work, as at the beginning of most of his Epistles, there was certainly prayer, entreaty, intercession, and thanksgiving for the young community. To the usual—and by no means erroneous—picture of Paul as the active, caring, suffering, disputatious missionary must be added that of the apostle in constant prayer. Paul was conscious that he worked not for his own sake, but for the cause of God. Without God's Spirit he and the young community could achieve nothing. It is certain, therefore, that Paul from the start exhorted the community to pray and to await the return of the Lord. We are reminded of this in the *maranatha*-call at the end of the first Epistle (16.22). Paul specifically tells the Corinthians—probably in connection with preparation for baptism—that he has passed on to them the tradition of faith in 1 Cor. 15.3b–5. For him, the converted Pharisee, the events of the crucifixion must have been quite repugnant, even before he had come to the turning point in his life. Thereafter, in his theological thinking, he must frequently have been concerned with the death on the cross. Yet neither in his missionary sermons nor in the preparation he gave for baptism, was he likely to have concentrated as exclusively on the crucifixion as he states retrospectively in 1 Corinthians. He preached and taught the message of Christ in much the same manner as was done in the traditional hymns and credal formulae: Christ, the Lord, who died for us, was raised and is now present, and the worshipping community is looking forward with joy to his imminent return.

Apart from baptizing the first converts, Paul obviously left baptism to others (1.14ff), probably to his fellow workers or even to the first converts, like Stephanas, who had become leaders of the community (1.16; 16.15ff). Although Paul adapted his missionary message to the modes of life and thought of the people he addressed it to, he did not—without qualification—become 'a Greek to the Greeks' as is so often misinterpreted from the above-mentioned passage. The canon of his missionary work was not cultural adaptability, but to gain followers for the gospel. This led him to a degree of solidarity with his audience, but not to complete adaptation to it. Paul did not become a Greek, nor a man without law, but 'as one outside the law—not being without law toward God but under the law of Christ—that I might win those outside the law' (1 Cor. 9.21). This closeness to the Gospel, which imparts a freedom that is limited only by love, shaped Paul's entire life. He endeavoured from the start to show the community that they, too, could share in this holding fast to Christ, and that their salvation depended on it (15.2). He was evidently successful in this, for belief in Christ became firmly established in the community at Corinth (3.10), nor was there any lack of spiritual gifts (1.6ff).

ii *The Dangers of Spiritual Enthusiasm*

After his departure from Corinth, the apostle wrote at least four letters to the community there, partly in answer to questions from Corinth and partly in response to disturbing news that reached him from there. Have the first letter, mentioned in 1 Cor. 5.9ff, and the 'letter of tears', mentioned in 2 Cor. 2.4; 7.8, been lost? Or are the Epistles to the Corinthians, as we now know them, the work of a later redactor who cast the entire Corinthian correspondence—consisting of at least four, possibly seven letters—into their present form, with their frequent changes from one subject to another? This question has been hotly disputed, but need not be gone into here, since we are examining a text which is firmly anchored within the context of 1 Cor. 1.10—4.21 and can be understood from this context. As a preliminary working hypothesis, it is assumed that the first Epistle to the Corinthians, at any rate, represents a homogeneous literary unit. Thus we have before us Paul's second letter to the Corinthians which was probably dictated in response to various reports and questions that had reached him from Corinth. It is likely that dictation was interrupted, hence the jumps from thought to thought and the breaks in the narrative flow. If this assumption is correct, the events that took place between the time the community was founded in about A.D. 51 or 52 and the time the Epistle was dictated at Ephesus, probably in the spring of A.D. 55 or 56, may be imagined as follows:

The community consisted of a minority of semitic and a majority of gentile Christians who had originally been recruited from among the worshippers of God who were connected with the synagogue at Corinth. While some members of the community were rich, the majority probably came from the class of paupers, slaves, and port workers—'not many' who 'were wise according to worldly standards . . . powerful' or 'of noble birth' (1 Cor. 1.26). From 1 Cor. 7.17–24 and 11.17–34 we can conclude that the diverse religious and social origins of the community's members soon led to problems and grievances.

More important, though, was the fact that Corinth, as an environment, obviously had a strong influence on the community. It was no accident that Paul used sporting terms in his letters to the Christians in the home of the Isthmian Games (1 Cor. 9.24ff). Daily contact with followers of other religions and with the representatives of a—partly religiously based—libertine life-style, created problems. This is clear from the questions regarding food offered to idols (1 Cor. 8; 10.23ff) and sexual morality (1 Cor. 5—7). Paul had evidently written about this in his first, misunderstood letter (5.9–13).

Graver in the long term than the problems arising from social differences and from the environment of Corinth, were the questions of faith, possibly stemming from a misunderstanding of Paul's teaching. The community had not been left entirely to its own devices. For a time Apollos, a Christian Jew from Alexandria, had continued Paul's missionary work. He was 'an eloquent man and well versed in the scriptures' (Acts 18.24ff). It has frequently been assumed that this native of Alexandria had preached a special gospel of Wisdom, shaped by gnostic ideas, and that this had created difficulties in Corinth. But not every Christian from Alexandria was a Christian Philo, and this assumption can certainly not be obtained from the first Epistle to the Corinthians. On the contrary, Paul writes with gratitude about Apollos's work (3.4ff), and asked him several times to return to Corinth (16.12). Perhaps, after Paul and Apollos, Peter too visited Corinth—although this remains improbable. The difficulties which arose in Corinth cannot, in my opinion, be explained by tensions between Paul and Peter, which are referred to in Galatians 2.

When the first Epistle to the Corinthians was written, there were no parties or groups centred on any particular individual in Corinth, but it may be said that their existed various groups of partisans. Paul in 1.10ff therefore did not use the word *hairesis*, or 'party', but *schisma*, 'division', 'dissension', and *eris*, 'quarrel', 'discord'. There was a 'puffing up' in favour of one against the other—Paul, Apollos, Cephas, or even Christ (1.12; 4.6). In his letter, therefore, Paul addresses the whole community and not this or that 'party'.

The immediate cause for writing was the disturbing news from Corinth brought by 'Chloe's people' (1.11): quarrels, dissension, and—stemming from these—even arguments against the apostle himself. An echo of these polemics can be heard in the words 'wisdom' and 'power', and in the passwords of 1.12. The memory of the apostle's 'weak' appearance at Corinth may also have played a part, and it was implied that even in his elementary teachings (2.1–4; 3.1–3) Paul had, after all, been weak. Thus he was criticized and also accused that, although he had promised to return to Corinth, he had not kept his word (4.18–21). It is possible that the polemics against Paul erupted in connection with the letter from the community, mentioned in 7.1. Those who were 'for Paul' would then have been those who urged a letter to Paul, among them possibly the delegation mentioned in 16.17. But others would have contradicted them: 'Why should we still turn to Paul? If we have to seek advice, then let us ask the learned Apollos! Even better, let us ask Peter! Since we belong to Christ and partake of his Spirit, we are well able to decide such questions ourselves!'

Paul had recognized that the gospel, and with it the salvation of the community, were at stake. Since the community could not grow into union with Christ without an intermediary, without apostolic teaching of the gospel, Paul's first concern was to restore confidence between the community and himself. 1 Cor. 1—4 might thus be termed an apologia of apostolic service. Not only confidence in the 'father' of the community was disturbed (4.14–16), but also the confidence of the Corinthian Christians in each other, and this threatened to divide Christ himself (1.13). Hence the repeated exhortations to unite (1.10–13; 3.3–4; 3.21–3). But behind the polemics and the resulting disputes, Paul recognized the sources of evil: a belief based on human wisdom (2.5), judgement still too much influenced by the spirit of the world (2.12), and an immature comprehension of Christ (3.1). In the first chapter of his letter to the Corinthians, Paul could therefore not confine himself to an apologia of apostolic service and exhortations to unity, but had to continue the missionary work begun at Corinth. In this Epistle he was not obliged to do battle with adversaries or infiltrators who preached a different gospel, as in the second Epistle, but had to wrestle with the community for a more profound understanding of the gospel.

It would therefore be erroneous to speak of a 'Corinthian theology' which the apostle rejected, since it can hardly have been a case of a thought-out gnostic system. The assumption that the Corinthians had developed the doctrine of a 'wisdom' christology, based on a personification of wisdom—known both to Greeks and Jews, as well as to the gnostics—is, in my view, improbable. Equally, the Corinthians' quest for wisdom cannot simply be equated with Greek philosophy.

For all their spiritual gifts, the slaves and port workers of Corinth, who had so recently been converted to Christianity, had had neither the time nor sufficient distance from their experience of conversion to think through their beliefs in such a way as to allow them to develop their own theology or to adopt another. But their spiritual enthusiasm had led them to a completely one-sided understanding of the tradition of faith (1 Cor. 15.3b–5) that had been passed on to them: Only the risen Lord matters; he gives us wisdom and power; already we are filled, already we are rich, already we may rule as in the Kingdom to come! (4.8) The Corinthians appeared to live in enthusiastic anticipation of the Kingdom. This spiritual

71

experience was combined with reflection on texts in the Old Testament and in intertestamental books (cf. section iv). Ideas gleaned from popular Greek philosophy, mystery religions, and from gnosticism, which was then developing, may also have played their part. In this way the spiritual experience threatened to be turned into a mere experience of self.

Into this situation Paul preached the gospel anew. While wrestling with the community for the right belief, he himself found new formulations and gained new insights. This will be demonstrated in a short passage from his impassioned argument, i.e. 1 Cor. 1.18–25.

iii *The One-sided Word of the Cross*

'Christ has sent me to proclaim the message of salvation, the Gospel of the crucified and risen Lord.' Thus Paul might have summarized his apostolic mission. But when this Gospel was misunderstood, as in Corinth, it could no longer be preached in a general way, as in the credal formula of 1 Cor. 15.3b–5. It was now necessary to write differently, more pointedly, polemically, one-sidedly. The essence of the gospel, in the Corinthian case, was 'Christ on the Cross'. Missionary service now meant to ensure that this central truth was not 'emptied of power' and rendered senseless, emasculated, and ineffective (1.17). The gospel = 'the word of the cross', that is the bold equation contained in the text we are about to examine (1 Cor. 1.18–25). Its literal translation runs as follows:

> (18a) The word of the cross:
> (18b) for those who are perishing
> is folly
> > (18c) but to us who are being saved
> > it is the power of God!
> > (19a) For it is written,
> (19b) I will destroy the wisdom of the wise
> (19c) and the cleverness of the clever I will thwart.
> (20a) Where is the wise man? Where is the scribe?
> Where is the debater of this age?
> (20b) Has not God made foolish the wisdom of the world?
> (21a) For since, in the wisdom of God, the world did not know God through wisdom,
> (21b) it pleased God through the folly of what we preach to save those who believe.

(22a) For Jews demand signs   (22b) and Greeks seek wisdom,
       (23a) but we preach
          Christ crucified
(23b) a stumbling block to Jews   and folly to Gentiles,
       (24a) but to those who are called,
    both Jews   and Greeks
             Christ
    the power of God   and   the wisdom of God.
(25a) For the foolishness of God is wiser than men,
(25b) and the weakness of God is stronger than men.

The Corinthians 'puffed themselves up' and fought each other with conflicting passwords and by adopting partisan positions. They sought to find the 'wisdom of the word', which Paul countered with his 'word of the cross'. This message of the cross is a paradox.

The paradox becomes apparent already in the idiom, in the *style* of the text. At Corinth Paul had deliberately preached his message without eloquence, in order not to empty Christ's cross of power (1.17; 2.1–5). The Corinthians, in their quest for 'word wisdom', blamed him for this. But it is in the nature of the cross that it cannot be preached elegantly and brilliantly, only in weakness. Yet now, paradoxically, Paul is endowed with poetic powers of speech: with a conciseness that can hardly be equalled, he now sets one keyword over against another. Just as a great painter on canvas defines the appearance and essence of a person with a few brush strokes, Paul defines in two or three words the human situation, God's plan of salvation, and the transformation of all values on Christ's cross. Even in the *form* of the statement its *content* is realized: those who completely and utterly hold fast to the weakness and folly of the crucifixion, will receive the gift of divine power and of God's wisdom.

The text is antithetic throughout. But it is important for the proper understanding of it that its *basic antithesis* be recognized. The Jews, who demand signs, are contrasted with the Greeks, as representatives of all the people who seek wisdom. This difference, however, is not ultimately decisive. Both are men (v. 25), both can be called by God to service and salvation (v. 24). Even the antitheses of wisdom/folly, power/weakness are not decisive factors, since what in the end will be revealed as wisdom or power, or by contrast as folly or weakness, will not be determined by immanent criteria, but by God's act of salvation. Nor is the kernel of the text to be looked for in the antithesis between those who perish and those who are saved (v. 18), since the definite decision still remains open. Paul shows the Corinthians that their search for wordly wisdom and their consequent disregard for the cross leads to ultimate perdition, but at the same time he still includes them in the 'us' and 'we' of vv. 18 and 23. The judgement as to who will be saved and who will perish is God's alone, and anything men may think about this is dependent upon this divine prerogative. The basic antithesis, which is the key to the entire text, is between God and men, between the extraordinary acts of God ('the word of the cross') and the actions of this world and age ('the wisdom of the world').

Who is this God who stands over against the world? In the difficult v. 21a—which is a preliminary form of Rom. 1.18ff—Paul maintains that we can recognize God and his wisdom in this world. Paul is probably employing concepts obtained from Jewish speculations on wisdom: according to a speech on wisdom contained in the aprocryphal book of Jesus son of Sirach (24.3), God's creative wisdom had surrounded the earth like a mist. In the midst of this wisdom of God, the world, i.e. mankind, might have been able to recognize God, guided by God's wisdom. But this the world had not done and still does not do, as is shown by the Corinthians' self-important search for wordly wisdom. God had therefore decided to choose a new path towards man that was both amazing and offensive (v. 21b). Only by reflection on Scripture in the light of the crucifixion (vv. 19–20; cf. also section iv below) were Paul's eyes opened to God's amazing decision: to save the believers by crucifying the Messiah! This message of folly is the message of joy. In our most extreme weakness we meet God!

Jews and Greeks, mankind in general, contradict the cross. In his struggle for the right faith with the community of Corinth, Paul does not dwell at all on Corinthian catchwords or partisan points of view, nor does he take sides. The groups who adhere to Paul, Apollos, Peter, or Christ are all of them merely examples of men who do not recognize or acknowledge God, because they do not look for him on the cross, nor in the weakness of dying. But Paul does distinguish between Jews and Greeks, since both have different concepts of God and are therefore by-passing the cross—and thus the real God—for different reasons. Those, who, like the Jews, worship God as a mighty king, wish to see signs of his power; they must therefore reject the cross as something obnoxious. Those, who, like the Greeks, see in God the all-embracing world principle, want to attain wise understanding of life and the world through such belief; they must therefore despise as folly the linking of God with the crucifixion of a Palestinian rebel. However different the reasons for their preconceptions and for their rejection of the word of the cross, both look for proofs of God, and both presume to judge God by their own criteria. Both attitudes constitute a negation of the cross, which to both is a stumbling block or a folly. Therefore, too schematic a linking of 'signs' and 'stumbling block' with the Jews, and of 'wisdom' and 'folly' with the Greeks would be pointless. Already in 1 Corinthians 1.18–25 and in the ensuing chapter a shift of emphasis can be detected: at first the issue is the Corinthians' search for wisdom, but then the emphasis is on God who is powerful in *weakness*.

Despite this contradiction, Paul exhorts the Corinthians to join him in preaching Christ as the crucified (the 'we' in v. 23 can be understood as such exhortation), for *the cross becomes the crisis of the world*. For all men, Jews and Greeks alike, it may be impossible to meet the true God in the crucified Jesus Christ. But Paul and the Corinthians have experienced for themselves that God may call men, give them faith and thus salvation. Hence the word of the cross must continue to be preached to all men—salvation to some, perdition to others. It is the word of the cross that creates this division (cf. 2 Cor. 2.14–16; 4.3–4). Yet Paul does not stress this division, nor the fate of the unbelievers, but only emphasizes the power of the word of the cross among believers.

To believers the cross means rescue, salvation. Yet it is probably no accident that Paul, in v. 24, does not address the Corinthians as 'those being saved' (v. 18c) or 'believers' (v.

21b), but as 'those who are called'. The word of *the cross is a call*: in vv. 26ff. this concept is adopted to demonstrate the existential meaning this call possesses both for the community (vv. 26–31) and for the apostle (2.1–5).

Not only for Christ, but equally for the community and for his apostles, God chooses the repugnant path into weakness. 'God chose what is weak in the world' (v. 27). Christian life is shaped by the fact that the true God can only be met at the cross, and Paul points to this existential interpretation in many passages of his Epistles.

In 1 Cor. 1.18–25 another aspect of the call, contained in the word of the cross, is emphasized, and this is without doubt the most important statement in the entire pericope. *The cross becomes the criterion* because God can be, and demands to be, recognized through it. Mankind might have recognized God through wisdom, but failed to do so. Therefore God had destroyed this—intrinsically possible—line of communication (vv. 19–21), to make way for another possibility of communication between himself and men: the cross. Through it all values are transformed: God's weakness is God's power, the foolish message of the cross is God's wisdom (v. 24). Jews and Gentiles can after all find what they have searched for so ardently, but they find it where they least expect it—at Golgotha. From here a completely new perspective is opened on all that happens among men (v. 25). The Corinthians judge their brethren and even Christ from their own point of view, by their own passwords and criteria. Now they are told to learn to judge themselves, their brethren, their age, and the world around them through the cross.

iv *Scripture, Tradition, Interpretation*

In all his arguments in 1 Cor. 1—3, Paul repeatedly refers to certain passages in Scripture. It is possible that in doing this he was using a collection of Jewish texts that warn against Greek wisdom, which he had learned by heart during his rabbinical studies at Jerusalem. If such a collection did exist and Paul was familiar with it, it is none the less unlikely that he had it to hand when dictating his first Epistle to the Corinthians. Quotations are from memory and there are also a number of allusions to certain passages. The list of quotations and allusions is as follows:

1 Cor.	OT	Reference
1.19	Isa. 29.14	quotation
1.19	Ps. 33.9	verb only
1.20	Isa. 19.11–12	allusion
1.20	Isa. 33.18	allusion
1.20	Isa. 44.25	allusion
1.31	Jer. 9.22–3	clear allusion
2.9	Test. Jam.?	quotation; echoes of Isa. 52.15; 64.3
2.16	Isa. 40.13	quotation
3.19	Job 5.12–13	quotation
3.20	Ps. 94.10	quotation

This relatively frequent use of the Old Testament shows that Paul, in line with the customs of the early Church, examined his perception of God's act of salvation through Christ by referring to Scripture. It also shows that reflection on Scripture was assidously practised at Corinth, but that there it had led only to an enthusiastic search for wisdom and signs. Which passages from the Old Testament and intertestamental literature may have played a role in this?

The Corinthian 'proof texts' are probably to be looked for in the Old Testament and more particularly in intertestamental wisdom literature. In the eighth chapter of Proverbs and in Job 28 we already find the concept of pre-existing wisdom. It had also played a part in creation, and now, personified, wisdom preaches and looks for those who will heed her (Prov. 1.20ff). This concept was developed much further in intertestamental writings (Sir. 24 and the strange fragment of wisdom in Eth. En. 42). Wisdom's search for disciples, and the search for those with insight for wisdom, was linked—especially in the Wisdom of Solomon—with God's purpose of salvation: wisdom reveals and leads the way. Wisdom takes those who heed her away from sin and godlessness and makes them whole (Wis. 4.7ff). In Proverbs this process of union had already been described, employing sexual symbolism (Prov. 9.1–6); wisdom is the bride of her pupil (Prov. 4.6ff). This union was also strongly stressed in intertestamental literature: 'She (wisdom) will come to meet him (who fears the Lord) like a mother, and like the wife of his youth she will welcome him. She will feed him with the bread of understanding, and give him the water of wisdom to drink. He will lean on her and will not fall, and he will rely on her and will not be put to shame. She will exalt him above his neighbours, and will open his mouth in the midst of the assembly.' (Sir. 15.2–5; cf. also Wis. 6.12–14; 8.2; 8.9.)

Who becomes as one with wisdom in this way, will also become as one with God, or at least with the image of God, and be filled with his Spirit. While the authors of the books of Sirach and Baruch saw the epitome of all wisdom in Jewish law, the Christians of Corinth saw the risen Christ, who was now present in the Holy Spirit, as the personification of wisdom. Small wonder that, by their union with him—in line with the Sirach text quoted above—they felt 'exalted above all neighbours' and 'opened their mouths in the assembly'. But they had little interest in Jesus the man and his way to the cross. They had left the cross far behind.

Paul is of quite a different opinion: communion with Christ can only be with Christ crucified. Taking up Corinthian catchphrases, the apostle shows his community how immature they are in their puffing up and how foolish in their quest for wisdom. He, too, supports his arguments by reference to Jewish wisdom literature. It has been shown earlier that in v. 21a Paul probably adopted concepts from Sirach. Like most New Testament authors, however, he seeks his 'key texts' in Isaiah and Jeremiah, in the prophecies of God's further acts to save the world.

The main text quoted in this connection is Isa. 29.14, but it is rendered in a form different from both the Hebrew and Septuagint texts. Paul's exegesis more resembles that of the Qumranites: viewed in the light of the crucifixion, God has allowed the wisdom of the wise men and the discernment of the discerning to perish, and not just 'hidden' it as in the Septuagint. And the subsequent explanatory verse 21b shows that God has taken an entirely new initiative. The wisdom of God, after an unsuccessful search for a home among men, has not retired to heaven (Eth. En. 42), but come to men in a 'foolish' way: in the weakness of the cross.

This scriptural meditation opened up new perspectives for Paul in his interpretation of the crucifixion. There are of course also echoes here and there of the early Church's traditional interpretation, but Paul leaves out the early Church's central element and aims traditional statements, as well as his own new interpretation, specifically at the situation of Corinth:

(1) The old credal formulae announce that 'Christ has died for our sins according to the scriptures'. Paul does not repeat 'for us'. Instead, he replaces the more general word 'died' by the offensive word 'crucified'. In this pointed abbreviation, the word of the cross becomes the entire gospel. The 'sins' are now concrete: they lead to a self-important search for wisdom, to dissension among the brethren, to the division of Christ. The saving death on the cross is now proclaimed in its decisive eternal significance: it is a question of eternal perdition or salvation.

(2) The early Christian interpretation, derived from psalms of lament and praise, preached the 'must' of the suffering righteous one's crucifixion. In v. 21 this 'must' is not only stated, but interpreted as a new initiative by God. It is significant that there follows no statement about the triumph of the suffering righteous, and there is not the slightest allusion to Christ's resurrection. The Corinthians have to learn to recognize God's power and wisdom not in the resurrection, but in the midst of the misery and folly of the crucifixion.

(3) The early Church's interpretation of the crucifixion as judgement and turning point in 1 Cor. 1.18ff is not portrayed as a cosmic apocalypse, but interpreted much more directly as a 'human apocalypse'. All preconceptions of God and his ways (and that includes all civilizations, religions, and theologies) fail. On the cross, and only there, eternal fate is decided: whoever rejects or accepts faithfully the folly of the message of the cross, also abandons or receives eternal salvation.

With his *ad hoc* interpretation for the Corinthians of old crucifixion traditions, based on his reflection on Scripture, Paul created a new tradition. Indeed, the meaning of the crucifixion had never before been interpreted as in 1 Cor. 1.18ff, not even by Paul himself. What the apostle, in his passionate wrestling for the right belief, dictated especially for the Corinthians, has gained ecumenical importance. Even during dictation, in the middle of the perfectly concrete context of 1 Cor. 1.10–17 and 1.26ff, Paul broadened the implications of his statements: for him the Corinthian situation typified that of the world in general, and thus the Corinthian Christians appear merely in the all-embracing 'us' and 'we'. Hence, what the apostle stated in a one-sided and *ad hoc* fashion, may now be taken as the valid interpretation of the crucifixion for the Church of all continents and all ages.

In this context it is essential that the Church of today also learns to use the cross as the criterion, because it is through the cross that God wishes to be perceived. Paul's most central contribution to the theology of the cross was not this or that interpretation of the event of the crucifixion, but his recognition that the faithful must interpret themselves and the entire world through the crucifixion.

2   For the Galatians: the Cross as Justification

It cannot have been an easy task to be Paul's secretary while he dictated his letter to the Galatians. The apostle was enraged, and his impetuous dictation could not have been transferred fast enough onto the scroll. The dispute starts already with the first sentence: 'Paul, an apostle—*not* (sent) from man nor (appointed) through man, but through Jesus Christ . . .' (1.1). Where in other Pauline letters the prescript is followed immediately by a prayer of thanks, praise, and intercession, in his Epistle to the Galatians, Paul can only voice his astonishment that they have so quickly deserted God for another gospel (1.6). The prayer is even replaced here by a twice-repeated anathema (1.8 and 9).

i   Crisis in Galatia

What had prompted this apostolic rage? This question is usually answered by pointing out that preachers proclaiming another gospel had entered the Galatian communities. The

literature on this subject expands annually, producing a
bewildering number of hypotheses. Were they emissaries sent
by Peter and James from Jerusalem, or were they representatives of the 'false brethren' mentioned in 2.4? Is it possible
that Paul had to fight on two fronts simultaneously, against
Judaists on the one hand and libertine hotheads on the other?
Were the adversaries judaizing gentile Christians or gentile
Christian gnostics? Were they proselytes who became Christians later, which would mean that they were not outsiders, but
members of the Galatian community? Or were they Jewish
Christians after all? In that latter case, what was the origin of
their message? Were they pharisaic preachers of the law,
Jewish Christian gnostics, or syncretists who had come under
the spell of the cult of Cybele of Asia Minor? Were they
people who had amalgamated Jewish theology with some
cosmic myth? Were they perhaps Qumranites or Jewish
Christians who had fled Palestine because of the Zealot
uprisings, or were they preachers of some kind of ideal of
sanctity?

The mere enumeration of these hypotheses leads one to
suspect that it is impossible to elucidate this question. We
know these preachers only from Paul's polemics, and it
cannot be excluded that the apostle misunderstood his adversaries, or, in his excitement, misconstrued their meaning. The
question as to who were the adversaries becomes less important as soon as one realizes that Paul's main concern was not
to rout the other preachers, but to confront the Galatians
themselves. There is the occasional swipe at adversaries, who
are never named (1.6ff; 4.17; 5.10, 12; 6.12ff), yet the letter's
main aim is not polemics, but the apostolic struggle that the
foolish and bewitched Galatians (3.1), who are about to fall
from grace (5.4), might find again their belief in the crucified
Lord and continue in their undivided faith in the Spirit they
have received. 'My little children, with whom I am again in
travail until Christ be formed in you!' (4.19). For the
interpretation of the Letter to the Galatians it is therefore not
important what the adversaries preached, but what the
Galatians heard of this sermon. In missionary situations
especially, there is often a considerable gap between what is
preached and what is received. Whence the adversaries came

81

and what they preached is thus not essential for the understanding of this letter. Much more important are the reasons—stemming from their religious and cultural background and their situation—why the Galatians 'so quickly' deserted the gospel preached by Paul, for the message, rightly or wrongly construed, of his adversaries.

What was it that the Galatians had heard and understood, and against which Paul wrote his most impassioned letter? They had not abandoned belief in the crucified Christ, nor did they doubt the soteriological significance of his death. But through the pressures brought to bear on them by Paul's adversaries, they had come to the conviction that only those who are circumcised can be certain of salvation (2.3; 5.2ff; 5.6; 6.12ff; 6.15). Only those were in the true sense sons of Abraham (3.6–18; 3.29). The issue was not so much the observance of all Jewish law, but the proper comprehension of Christian freedom. What evidently exercised the Galatians most was the question of how this freedom which Paul had preached was to be lived in daily life (Gal. 5 and 6, and particularly 6.1ff). They were therefore inclined to accept from the adversaries' message certain injunctions of the law (2.11—4.31; 4.21; 5.4); probably not only circumcision, but also the observance of certain days, months, seasons, and years (4.10). This resolve was further strengthened by their own interpretation of Scripture (cf. section (iii) below). Hand in hand, for Paul, with the Galatians' acceptance of some of the teachings of the adversaries, which complemented his own, went a crisis of his authority. Certainly this was in part caused, or exacerbated, by the adversaries' polemics against him (1.1,12; 1.10; 2.2ff; 5.11); but beyond that, the Galatian Christians evidently had questions to which Paul had given no answer, while his adversaries had provided concrete ones.

ii The Problems of Converted Barbarians

Can this crisis be explained by the Galatians' cultural and religious background? In this connection, just as in the question of who were the adversaries, we can only make assumptions. The whereabouts of the Galatia of the Epistle is, for instance, still under dispute. Was it the Roman province of Galatia, which had existed since 25 B.C. and comprised, apart from the region of Galatia in central Asia Minor, Pisidia, Lykaonia, parts of Phrygia, and Isauria, as well as Pamphylia? In that case, the letter might have been addressed to the community in the south of the province, which Paul had founded on his first missionary journey and had revisited at the start of his second journey. The recipients would thus have been Christians living in Pisidian Antioch and Iconium, Lystra, and Derbe in Lykaonia (Acts 13.13–14; 28; 16.1). More probable than this hypothesis as to the whereabouts of Galatia, is the assumption that the letter had been addressed to the 'disciples' who had been converted in the *region* of Galatia during the second mission and revisited during the third. It is this latter supposition, that by Galatia was meant the *region*, which is nowadays accepted by most scholars.

According to this, the Galatians were Hellenized Celts (Gallians). Their military excursion south-eastwards from the area between the Rhine and Danube had antedated the great migration. As early as 279 B.C. they had reached Macedonia. From there they proceeded simultaneously to Thrace, Asia Minor, and Greece, and only when they had reached Delphi were they forced to retreat. The Galatians who had been defeated in Thrace united with those who had retreated from Delphi, and later followed other Galatian tribes, who had already crossed the Hellespont. In the service of various kings, the Galatian mercenaries became the dreaded scourge of Asia Minor. Only after several defeats was it possible to force these barbarians to abandon their raids and settle within the region of Galatia. There they continued to remain autonomous, and only from 183–166 were they a province of the kingdom of Pergamum. In 25 B.C., after the death of the Galatian king Amyntas, the major part of Asia Minor became a Roman province, with Ankyra (the present Ankara) as its capital. At the time of Paul, the Galatians had become quite Hellenized, especially those of Pergamum. There must have been some syncretism of old Celtic cults and the religion of the indigenous Phrygian population of Galatia. For example, in Roman times half of all priestly positions at the sanctuary of Cybele, in the west-Galatian town of Pessinus, were held by Celts. Games were held in Ankyra in honour of Aesculapius, and the Roman emperor cult was also widespread. For all that, exegesis, in my view, has overplayed the extent to which the Galatians had become Hellenized. When Paul had interrupted his journey through Galatia because of illness (4.13ff), and had preached the gospel to the Celtic barbarians, he crossed a greater cultural barrier than in his later missionary work in the Greek towns of Philippi, Athens, and Corinth. The Galatians had always made common cause with the Romans against the Hellenic princes, and thus the process of their Hellenization was curbed by Roman influences. Just as in Roman Gaul, it is most likely that in Galatia, too, the old Celtic idols continued to be worshipped under another name. Even at the time of Hyronimus, the country people of Galatia spoke Celtic, and in Christian Galatia old Celtic customs survived, as for example the public feasts given to the population by generous priests which recall an ancient custom of the Celtic chieftains. This particular religious and cultural background of the Galatians must be taken into account when interpreting the Epistle to the Galatians.

It is probably no accident that some hundred years after this Epistle, many of the Christians there became Montanists. This heresy, which combined Christian tenets with the most rigorous asceticism, probably answered questions of the Galatians similar to those which the adversaries and Paul in his subsequent letter had tried to respond to. The Galatians had heard the sermon of the crucified Christ with faith, and had therefore received the Spirit (3.1–5). In his letter, Paul reminds them repeatedly of the crucial event of their receiving the Spirit. He is able to address them as 'spirituals', as 'pneumatics' (6.1). They had also richly experienced the Spirit's power of miracle and prayer (3.5; 4.6) and had thus been given an entirely new being (3.27; 6.15). The former divisions were abolished (3.26–8), as was the former bondage to elemental spirits (4.8–9). The Galatians experienced this transformation as a decisive liberation. In the course of missionary history, all that the Celtic barbarians experienced through the message of the Gospel has happened time and again to other peoples, who were frequently in bondage to the powers of nature. The crisis in Galatia has thousands of counterparts in missionary history.

After an initial period of spiritual enthusiasm and of an all-transcending experience of salvation and liberation, there follows a time when the newly converted are faced with the realities of self-seeking human nature, as yet unguided by the Spirit. Paul called this human nature, which is left to itself, *sarx*, a concept that can only inadequately be translated as 'flesh'. It was concrete problems like these deriving from *sarx* which lay behind the crisis in Galatia. How could spiritual men live without 'trespassing' against the will of God (6.1)? But if such trespasses occurred in a community—as was evidently the case in Galatia—did the Christians then not lose their salvation? To these questions Paul's adversaries, who had meanwhile come into Galatia, had concrete answers, and they evidently based their preaching on a particular interpretation of Scripture.

iii *Two Kinds of Reflection on Scripture*

We can no longer determine how Paul's adversaries actually interpreted Scripture. But how the Galatians understood their interpretation can be deduced from Paul's reactions: our salvation is indeed at stake, but not only because of our trespasses. More perilous for salvation is the freedom in Christ, which Paul had proclaimed, and of which the preachers who came after him said that this is 'man's gospel' (1.11), whereby Christ is made 'an agent of sin' (2.17). The promise of salvation through Christ, made to the people of Israel, is equally meant for us, who are called barbarians, but only if we become the sons of Abraham. That means we have to enter into a brotherhood in God with Israel, hence circumcision. It further means we must observe the law, because the promise made to Abraham, the brotherhood, and the law belong together. The law is not only Torah, as observed by the Jews, but the whole order of creation and the cosmic cycle, which God has made. This was what the preachers who came after Paul taught, based on apocalyptic texts and books of wisdom. Therefore, for the sake of our salvation, we must observe certain days, months, seasons, and years. On our observing such laws depends our being-in-Christ, our spirituality, and our partaking in the promised salvation.

Paul bluntly rejected this teaching as a 'different gospel' (1.6ff), and wrote to the Galatians that they were about to 'turn back again' to paganism (4.9). Indeed, the rightly or wrongly interpreted anti-Pauline preaching, and in particular its putative stress on the order of creation, might have induced (or as Paul says in 3.1 'betwitched') them to turn back to their elemental spirits and observe once again the feasts connected with their old myths.

If one wants to understand Paul's subsequent arguments correctly, it is first of all essential to appreciate when he dictated his letter and what stage the development of his theological thinking had reached. If the supposition that by Galatia was meant the region is correct, the letter is likely to have been written either towards the end of his stay at Ephesus, or more likely still in Macedonia, on his journey from Ephesus to Corinth (in the late autumn of 56 or 57, depending on when one fixes the chronological date of his sojourn at Ephesus). The many parallels, both of idiom and content, between it and the Corinthian and Roman letters, confirm this dating. The Letter to the Galatians was therefore written after the first Epistle to the Corinthians and not long before the Epistle to the Romans, at about the same time as several parts of the second Letter to the Corinthians. It can therefore be taken that the insights about the significance of the crucifixion which Paul had gained from his first dispute with the Corinthians informed the view he proclaimed to the Galatians. For him, the crucifixion was the criterion of his entire theological thinking, as it was for his interpretation of Scripture; while his thinking in regard to the role played by the law, and its justification, which he defined in his letter to the Romans, was still being developed. This obviously does not mean that only then did Paul begin to reflect about the law, about Christ's crucifixion, and about justification by faith. Even while still a Pharisee and a persecutor of Christians, these subjects had been central to his reflection on Scripture. But only from his argument with the Galatians did Paul gain his particular vision of the role of the Law and of justification through faith. In dictating his letter to the Galatians, he formulated these central insights of his theology for the first time, still quite crudely, radically, and one-sidedly, when contrasted with the balanced formulations of his later Roman Epistle.

In the first two chapters of Galatians, Paul demonstrates that he did *not* receive the gospel 'from man', but because he was called by God through Jesus Christ. By his own example he demonstrates the absurdity of the other preachers' teaching: he, the Jew by birth, zealous for the traditions of his fathers, advanced in the observance of Judaism beyond many of his own age, could nevertheless not be justified by works of law, in order to be justified by God and thus attain salvation (1.13—2.21). Towards the end of this introductory passage, where Paul states his position in regard to the crisis of his authority in Galatia, there is already an echo of the main theme in the subsequent chapter. Hence one might well consider that the second part of the Epistle opens with 2.15 instead of with 3.1, as is usually thought: 'For I through the law died to the law, that I might live to God. I have been crucified with Christ, it is no longer I who live, but Christ who lives in me; and the life I now live in the flesh I live by faith in the Son of God, who loved me and gave himself for me. I do not nullify the grace of God; for if justification were through the law, then Christ died to no purpose' (2.19ff).

This has an apodictic ring to it, as yet without any reference to Scripture, but with an echo of traditional credal formulae. First and foremost, however, it is a personal statement of faith, reflecting insights gained from his argument with the Corinthians. But that this is not merely an individual experience, but a typically Christian one, is made clear in the subsequent passage. The Galatians, too, have had such experience. They did not receive the Spirit and its miraculous powers by works of law, but by hearing with faith (3.1–5). In his preaching in Galatia, as in Corinth, Paul probably used traditional credal formulae, as for example 1 Cor. 15.3b–5. Now he summarizes the content of the gospel by a key word from his struggles with the Corinthian community for the right faith: 'Jesus Christ . . . crucified' (Gal. 3.1). Paul had thus portrayed him publicly to the Galatians; now they are enjoined to keep him before their eyes in their meditation on the Scriptures, since he is the key to the understanding of them.

The adversaries had evidently claimed not only that Paul received his gospel 'from man', but that it was 'a man's gospel' (1.11ff). Hence Paul is now obliged to demonstrate that his gospel is 'according to the scriptures'. He interprets the Old Testament concepts of 'promise', 'faith' and 'sons of Abraham' anew, that is to say, through Christ and towards Christ. Thus, for him, the Law acquires a new role. At this point only the beginning of his scriptural meditation will be briefly outlined (3.6ff).

Paul and the Galatians were not the first to be justified by faith in God, and can therefore be certain of their salvation. What the adversaries, who had invoked Abraham as their strongest witness, apparently did not know, the Scriptures, here almost personalized, knew long before: 'Abraham believed in God and it was reckoned to him as righteousness!' In this almost literal quotation from Genesis 15.6 in the Septuagint, Abraham's faith in God's promise and miraculous powers is commented upon: God judges that Abraham, because of his faith, is in the right relation to him. He is thus reckoned to be righteous. For Paul, therefore, he is not the circumcised man, nor the man to whom the land was promised, nor even the ancestor of Moses, but the archetype of the faithful. In the following v. 7, Paul goes a step further and takes up a catchphrase of his adversaries and a demand from the Galatians, which, by the way, the context of Gen. 15.6 also yields quite naturally: 'it is men of faith (who are righteous, but more) who are the sons of Abraham.' This is immediately underlined by a further word from Scripture about Abraham, and in Paul's formulation of v. 8 becomes a 'proto-gospel': 'in you shall all the (pagan) nations be blessed' (a compound Septuagint quotation from Gen. 12.3b and Gen. 18.18b). Being the sons of Abraham means entering into his inheritance, the blessing of God. As preached in the Gospel and as foreseen in the promise to Abraham, God's blessing is for all the nations, all who live in faith like Abraham, who had faith (v. 9). This is one side of the argument, the side of salvation.

In contrast to this, we have the other side, where 'curse' is the key word. Paul does not argue the continuity of the history of salvation. Using the method of rabbinical interpretation of Scripture, he combines quotations and thus constructs his argument. From his point of view there is no continuous line from Abraham to Moses and the Law, and thence to Christ and the community. The history of salvation, in its specific sense, for him begins only in Christ (4.4ff) and from that eschatological event of Christ, the Scriptures must be interpreted afresh. In this Paul departs from rabbinical exegesis, while continuing to employ its methods, and comes closer to the Qumranite manner of scriptural interpretation.

In the light of God's reality, as revealed through Christ, 'all who rely on the works of the law' are under a curse (v. 10a). Paul does not even pause to consider whether, at least in theory, it might be possible to fulfil the law and thereby to attain salvation. Quoting Deut. 27.26, he simply states 'cursed be every one who does not abide by all the things written in the book of the law and do them.' Paul, with this last of twelve curses in Deut. 27.15–26, refers to the entire law by transforming the specific statement 'the words of this law' into the more general 'all things written in the book of the law'. This conviction, that in fact no one can fulfil the entire law, Paul had gained from a Habakkuk prophecy, which he had interpreted in the light of Christ. The Hebrew text of this is: 'The righteous shall live by this belief/his faithfulness', which, in the intertestamental era—for instance in the Qumran community—was interpreted in the sense of being faithful to the law. According to the Septuagint, God said: 'The righteous shall live by my faithfulness', which might also be translated as: 'The righteous shall live by his faith/trust in me.' The Greek-Jewish proselytizing mission interpreted this occasionally as a call to believe in the *one* God. Paul omits the attributes 'his' or 'my', because his concern is with the key word 'faith/trust', which for him excludes the other side, the living by the works of the law. 'By the law' no one can be justified before God (v. 11). He categorically writes 'no one': neither the Jews who abide by the Torah, nor the Galatians who believe in the laws of creation. It is likely that Paul deliberately formulated this in the present tense: in this present crisis in Galatia, too, salvation is not to be attained by the laws of the Torah or the laws of creation.

Promise and Law, to live by faith or by the works of the law, are to each other as blessing and curse. 'The law does not rest on faith' (v. 12), it lives by observing it. But this observance is not only impossible for man, it also entices him to seek justification by the law. Thus the law becomes the curse for all. Having reached this dead end, a new understanding of Christ's death is opened up for Paul.

iv   Curse turned into Blessing

As in the passage 1 Cor. 1.18ff, which has already been discussed, Paul, in Gal. 3.13ff, sees Christ's crucifixion as a radical challenge to human thought and action. But now it is not the recognition of God through wisdom that is being challenged, but the human striving for salvation through justification by the law. Just as God, by his actions on the cross, has vanquished wisdom, so has he abolished the law as a path to salvation. Paul shows the Galatians how this happened. This also meant a new insight for the apostle. This is made evident by the fact that the same thought in a similar formulation also appears in the second Epistle to the Corinthians, which was dictated at about the same time.

Gal. 3.13ff	2 Cor. 5.20ff

'Christ redeemed us
from the curse of the law,
   having become
   a curse
   for us. . . .
that in Christ Jesus
the blessing of Abraham
might come upon the Gentiles.'
	'We beseech you on behalf of Christ,
	be reconciled to God.
	Him who knew no sin
	   he made
	   to be sin
	   for our sake,
	so that in him we might become
	the righteousness of God.'

Underlying these statements are the early Church's credal formulae about the soteriological meaning of Christ's death (cf. chapter 2, 3). Paul transmits the Church's credal tradition, but again in a way that gives an *ad hoc* interpretation for the Galatians and Corinthians in their crisis of faith.

Not only *that* Christ died for us, but *how* this 'for us' came about, becomes clear to Paul in his arguments with the community. He does not adopt the early Church's narrative crucifixion traditions in order to interpret the manner and the effect of Christ's death, as did the Evangelists later. He does not relate in narrative style that Christ became accursed or a sinner, but formulates abstractly and thus explains the manner and effect of Christ's death as dogma. If Paul, in his first letter to the Corinthians, for the first time clearly formulated the principles of his theological thinking, now in his dispute with the Galatians he states for the first time the dogmatic case of his theological thought: the cross as justification.

The law becomes the curse for all. Seen from the point of view of human possibilities, there is no way out, no way to salvation, to grace, to freedom. All are condemned to slavery—Jews, Greeks, and barbarians alike. This is how Paul sees the situation of 'the present evil age' (1.4). But in this hopeless situation he is able to preach the gospel: 'Christ has redeemed us!' As previously in 1 Cor. 6.20; 7.23; and later in Gal. 4.5, Paul uses a verb which was a well-known Greek trading term. It has often been assumed that it referred to the ritual ransoming of slaves, but the word does not appear as a technical term in any extant documents concerning the ransom of slaves. But there exists documentation for its meaning 'settling', 'satisfying'. Paul probably uses the verb in the general sense of 'saving', 'freeing', similar to the statement at the beginning of the letter, that Christ 'gave himself for our sins to deliver us from the present evil age' (1.4). In the gospel preached to the Galatians in Gal. 3.13ff, the main accent certainly does not lie on the image of the ransomed slave. Nor would it lead anywhere, in reading this passage, to speculate on who had to pay whom and for what, and who it was that had to be satisfied.

Reflection on Scripture opened up quite different perspectives for Paul. 'Cursed be every one who hangs on a tree.' The law which he quotes from Deut. 21.23 reads in its original Hebrew text as: 'a hanged man is accursed by God', while the Septuagint translates it as: 'accursed is every one who hangs on a tree.' What this sentence of the law meant to the ancient Israelites has already been explained in chapter 1, 1 (ii). It did not mean the crucifixion of a living man, but the hanging on a tree of a dead body that had already been executed, usually by stoning. In connection with the crucifixion of rebels in

91

Palestine, however, this 'pole' or 'tree' was equated with the cross, probably already in the intertestamental era and certainly at the time of the New Testament (cf. Acts 5.30; 10.39; 13.29; 1 Pet. 2.24). Thus the hanging on a tree could be (mis)understood as crucifixion. Paul, at least, interprets it this way in his free quotation from Deut. 21.23. Christ had been crucified and had therefore become accursed. Could Paul, as a Christian, really assume and maintain something as horrendous as this? Especially if we remember the Old Testament realities of blessing and curse, this statement in Gal. 3.13 appears to be blasphemous in the sense of 1 Cor. 12.3, rather than a statement of faith in Christ. Indeed, it is frequently assumed that Paul employed here some Jewish polemic against Christ—perhaps a catchphrase dating from the period when he himself still persecuted Christians. I believe it is more likely that Paul truly meant what he dictated: it is not only said that Christ had become accursed. Christ had not merely taken upon himself the curse that is on us. The qualification made in the parallel text of 2 Cor. 5.21a (who knew no sin) is missing in Gal 3.13. Christ had indeed become accursed for us. How can this be a message of salvation?

Explanations usually refer to the concept of 'vicarious-ness', but the issue is larger. It is not merely an exchange, but a mutual partaking in the fate of the other. Christ not only became accursed for us and in our place, but shared the human fate, so that we might share his fate. This becomes clear in the parallel passage of 2 Cor. 5.21, and in particular in Gal. 4.4ff, where Paul, often with identical words and turns of phrase, takes up the thoughts of 3.13ff and develops them:

Gal. 3.13ff	*Gal. 4.4ff*
'Christ redeemed us from the curse of the law, having become a curse for us ... that ... the blessing of Abraham might come upon the Gentiles, that we might receive the promise of the Spirit through faith.'	'But when the time had fully come, God sent forth his Son, born of woman, born under the law, to redeem those who were under the law, so that we might receive adoption as sons. ... God has sent the Spirit ...'

What is said in 3.13ff regarding the crucifixion and sonship of Abraham is enlarged in 4.4ff to include all of Christ's mission, beginning with his incarnation, and it also refers beyond Abraham to the sonship of God. In both passages Christ's partaking of the human fate has the effect of liberation, and both passages lead to the receiving of the Spirit. Christ became what we are in order that we may become what he is. He has not saved us as man's 'proxy', but as man's 'vicar'. Because he became what we are, we can now 'live to God' (2.19), 'put on Christ' (3.27), are 'set free' (5.1), and can 'walk by the Spirit' (5.16). Since, according to the insight contained in 1 Cor. 1.18ff, the folly of God was more powerful than the wisdom of man, and the weakness of God more powerful than all human power, the accursed Son of God is a greater grace than all human blessings.

From this—probably first—formulation of the core of his theological thought in the letter to the Galatians and the second letter to the Corinthians, Paul goes on to give his views about the problem which had prompted the crisis in Galatia: the living in the flesh according to the Spirit, which threatens constantly to revert to living in the flesh according to the flesh. In answer to this problem he cannot and will not preach observance of the Law as the ideal of sanctity, as presumably did the anti-Pauline preachers. From the justification of the accursed, perceived in 3.6ff, a much more radical solution is derived: 'those who belong to Christ Jesus have crucified the flesh (*sarx*) with its passions and desires' (5.24).

When this crucifixion of *sarx* is supposed to have happened is not defined in so many words. Potentially it happened for the Galatians with the crucifixion of Christ at Golgotha and became manifest with their baptism. But Paul does not use the passive form, as is usual in baptismal texts, but the active aorist. Therefore it is likely that Paul is directly alluding to the conversion of the Galatians, to their conscious acceptance that this means the death sentence on their former being. The sins belong to their former being, to the life according to the flesh, which has now been crucified. He who lives in the flesh according to the Spirit is not freed from all 'trespasses' (6.1), nor are the Galatians. But, in contrast to his argument with the Corinthians in his first Epistle, Paul does not emphasize these trespasses. The emphasis is rather on their being led only by the Spirit. As spiritual men, the faithful in their struggles with the flesh can withstand the temptations of evil, *if* they abide by the crucified Christ and by him alone.

It remains doubtful whether the Galatians understood this message, both obnoxious and liberating, that the accursed are justified by the cross, through Christ's becoming accursed. Did they dare, through their faith in this message, to live as completely by the Spirit as Paul had enjoined them to do? Whatever their case, at no age and in no civilization must this radical message of the cross, with its consequences for Christian life, go unheeded.

4

The Gospel of the Crucifixion: Interpretations of the Evangelists

'The Good News of Jesus Christ' was the title Mark gave to his Gospel, and with it created a novel literary form. This good news must always be told anew if it is to remain gospel. That this occurred already in the New Testament is shown by a comparison of the crucifixion narratives in the four canonic Gospels. Only if we are clear where the testimonies of the four evangelists coincide and where they differ can we recognize how each preserved the crucifixion traditions and transmitted and interpreted them in a special manner, and where each, in his good news of the crucified Christ, placed the main emphases.

1 The Crucifixion Narrative in Synoptic Comparison

i The Message as Narrative

Letters have dates, they bear the imprint of sender and recipient; they are frequently answers to specific questions and are thus aimed at a concrete situation. Letters must therefore be read in the context of their age and environment—which may be totally different from ours—and thus be interpreted from their origin. Tales, such as fairy stories or myths, by comparison, have an almost timeless quality. They have crossed cultural boundaries and centuries without losing much that is essential to their form or immediacy. Narratives can therefore be read more easily and directly as applicable also to our own world and age.

If we are to examine the interpretation of the crucifixion in the *narratives* of the four Evangelists, the difference I have just outlined between the two categories of narratives and letters—which latter were the subject of the previous chapter—must not be lost sight of. Yet it must be immediately added that the Gospels—and with them the passion narratives—constituted a completely novel form of literature as it then existed. Therefore, not all that is known about the literary category of 'narration' can be applied without qualification to the Gospels. For this reason, form-critical research was unable to fit the passion narratives, or indeed the Gospels as a whole, into any known literary category. Even the ancient Church had difficulty in finding a name for what Mark, Matthew, Luke, and John had written. Only at about A.D. 150 do we find that Justin gives the definition for these books as *evangelia*—a name by which they are still known in many languages. Before this, the secular meaning of the word was the good news of a victory, an enthronement, or an imperial birthday. In the Bible the concept was used for the prophecies of God's acts of salvation (thus as a verb in Deutero-Isaiah) and for salvation through Christ (in the New Testament).

Since the Gospels are narratives with a prophetic character, the literary distinctions that can be drawn between the passages in the Epistles which refer to the crucifixion and the crucifixion narrative in the Gospels are rendered relative.

The author of the Epistles, Paul, as well as the writers of the Gospels, referred to the same historical event, and they all took it for granted that this event was of paramount importance for the people of all nations and all ages. Their purpose was to bear witness to the crucified Christ; not just to answer questions by letter, to tell a tale, or to write history. Despite the epistolary character of 1 Cor. 1.18ff and Gal. 3.6ff, which Paul dictated *ad hoc*, these pericopes were not only addressed to the Christians of Corinth and Galatia, but to the Church of all ages and civilizations. It should not be overlooked, on the other hand, that despite the narrative character of the Gospels' crucifixion accounts, these passages, too, were partially influenced by the date of their writing, the redactor, and the situation of their original readers.

There exists a plethora of contemporary exegesis of redactional history, which examines the specific direction of the individual Gospels. The question being asked is how the narration responded theologically to specific situations. It must be said, though, that virtually nothing is known about the redactors of the Gospels. They are witnesses who have retreated almost completely behind their testimony. We also know much less about the first readers for whom the Gospels were written, than we do about the communities of Corinth or Galatia. Considering the topic of this book, this is particularly regrettable. When comparing the four crucifixion narratives, we *can* say that there are considerable variations and different theological emphases. However, since so little is known with certainty about the authors, or about the situation of the first readers, we can at most make assumptions as to *why* the crucifixion narrative was interpreted theologically by each of the Evangelists in a particular manner.

The crucifixion narrative is a sub-section of the passion story, which in turn is part of the Gospels. For the proper understanding of the crucifixion accounts it is important to remember this. It is impossible in what follows to take into consideration every text that concerns the passion; even individual exegesis of each of the four crucifixion narratives would be beyond the scope of the present study. Therefore only the following questions will be examined: What is the relation between the four crucifixion narratives (cf. section 1 (ii) below)? How does each of the Evangelists develop the early Church's reflection on Scripture in his crucifixion narrative and what can be deduced from this use of the Scriptures about his specific theological direction (cf. sections 2 (i), 3 (i), 4 (i) and 5 (i) below)? What is the specific theological direction of each of the four crucifixion narratives, and does this confirm or cast doubt on the results of several important studies of each of the four passion stories (cf. sections 2 (ii), 3 (ii), 4 (ii) and 5 (ii) below)?

ii *The Literary Connections between the Evangelists*

Nowhere else do the four Gospels coincide as closely as in the passion story. This is particularly true of the crucifixion narrative. Not only the so-called Synoptics, but John, too, can therefore usefully be set side by side in a synoptic comparison. The comparison shows that they share the following narrative structure:

	Matt. 27	Mark 15	Luke 23	John 19
Way to the cross	20b–1	31b–2	26–32	16–17a
Crucifixion	22–7	33–8	33–4	17b–24
Around the cross	29–32	39–44	35–43	26–7
Jesus's death	33–7	45–50	44–6	28–30
Signs and witnesses	38–41	51–6	47–9	31–7

If one compares the texts in greater detail, there immediately appear a wealth of divergences within this common structure. According to the explanatory synopsis in the appendix to chapter 4 (pp. 135–9), the relatively short crucifixion narratives have no less than twenty passages which contain special material, ten divergences from Mark's narrative structure, and, compared with his text, thirteen omissions, as well as divergences of style and content even in those verses where two, three, or all four Evangelists' accounts are parallel.

Even a casual glance at the synopsis shows that *Mark* and *Matthew* transmit the crucifixion story in a broadly similar way. Without divergences, they follow the same narrative structure, and apart from Matt. 27.51b–3, there is little special material contained in their texts. *Luke* has many parallels with Mark and Matthew, but also contains significant transpositions, important omissions, and much special material. *John*'s passion story, and also his crucifixion narrative, run parallel with the synoptic accounts to a much greater degree than other parts of his Gospel. There are many points of contact, especially with Luke, but also instances of remarkable congruity with Matthew as against Luke. With his many divergences from the structure of Mark/Matthew, his important omissions, and extensive special material, however, John follows his own separate path.

This first impression is confirmed by word-count (cf. pp. 101f). In discerning the literary affinities, one needs to go much further, though, than merely to establish the similarities of form and sequence of words by a word-count. Statistical synopsis can, however, confirm or cast doubt on impressions that have been gained from comparisons of literary style and composition. The following table takes Mark's text as the basis for comparison. The column headed Mark gives first the verse (V), followed by the number of words (NW) of the statement referred to. In the columns headed Matthew, Luke, and John, the verse is given first (V), followed by the number of words (NW) in the parallel statements of these Gospels, and thirdly the number of words that appear in identical form and sequence to Mark's text (Id.W). Special material is shown as S, and divergences from the Mark/Matthew sequence are indicated by darts ($\vee \wedge$).

How can the similarities and divergences that one observes in a synoptic comparison of structure and word-count be explained? What are the reasons for omissions and additions of special material which occur frequently, at least in Luke and John?

The majority of scholars assume that *Mark* not only wrote the first Gospel, but was also the first to combine the pre-canonic passion account(s) with other collections of traditions about Jesus's sayings and deeds. For the composition of his Gospel he had at his disposal one—or several—crucifixion narrative(s). It is also usually assumed that the other Evangelists, or at least the other synoptic Evangelists, were familiar with Mark's version. Indeed in his Gospel, compared with that of Matthew and Luke, there is very little special material, only about seven words in a crucifixion narrative comprising 307 words. (In this connection only new *scenes* are considered as special material, but not new *details* of scenes.)

In the opinion of most scholars, *Matthew* took Mark's crucifixion narrative and reworked it by redaction. But there exist divergences between the two that cannot be traced back purely to the redaction of Mark's text. Therefore it has also been assumed that the same rudimentary narrative crucifixion tradition had been available both to Mark and Matthew, and that each edited his own account of the crucifixion from this. The more likely hypothesis, however, is, in my view, that Matthew freely retold the Marcan crucifixion narrative which was probably read out during church services, but also used vivid oral traditions still extant. This hypothesis would explain why Matthew uses more than half of Mark's words in identical form and sequence (158 words of 307), and why the passages in Matthew which are parallel to those of Mark are of roughly equal length (315 and 300 words respectively). It would further serve to explain the origin of the special material contained in Matthew (fifty-six words).

Mark 15		Matt. 27			Luke 23			John 19		
V	NW	V	NW	IdW	V	NW	IdW	V	NW	IdW
20b	6	31b	6	2	26a	4	2	16b	4	0
21	19	32	14	6	26b	15	7	17a	5	2
–		–	–		27ff	90S	–	–	–	
22	12	33	11	5	33a	9	4	17b	10	1
23	9	34	12	3	–	–		–	–	
24a	3	35a	3	1	33b	3	2	18a	3	0
–		–	–		34a	12S	–	–	–	
24b	12	35b	6	5	34b	7	3	23f	67∨	3
–		36	5S	–	–	–		–	–	
25	7S	–	–		–	–		–	–	
26	12	37	17	6	38	11 ∨	6	19	21	4
–		–	–		–	–		20ff	53S	–
27	14	38	13	8	33c	11∧	4	18b	15∧	1
–		–	–		–	–		26f	39S	–
–		–	–		35a	5S	–	–	–	
29f	27	39f	32	23	–	–		–	–	
31a	11	41	11	9	35b	6	2	–	–	
31b	6	42a	6	6	35c	4	3	–	–	
32a	14	42b	12	8	35d	9	2	–	–	
–		43	15S		–	–		–	–	
32b	7	44	12	6	39a	16	1	–	–	
–		–	–		39bff	56S	–	–	–	
33	13	45	13	9	44	16	10	–	–	
–		–	–		45a	3S	–	–	–	
34	26	46	24	9	–	–		–	–	
35	9	47	11	6	–	–		–	–	
–		–	–		–	–		28	15S	–
36	18	48f	28	12	36	10∧	0	29	15	2
–		–			37	11S	–	–	–	
37a	6	50a	7	3	46a	7	2	–	–	
–		–	–		46b	8S	–	–	–	

Mark 15		Matt. 27			Luke 23			John 19		
V	NW	V	NW	IdW	V	NW	IdW	V	NW	IdW
	–		–	–		–	–	30a	9S	–
37b	1	50b	3	0	46c	4	1	30b	7	0
38	12	51a	13	10	45b	7∧	3	–	–	
	–	51bff.	36S	–		–	–	–	–	
39	20	54	24	4	47	16	6	–	–	
	–		–	–	48	16S	–	–	–	
40f.	43	55f.	37	17	49	18	4	25	24∧	3
	–		–	–			–	31ff.	107S	–
S	7	S		56	S		201	S		223
Mark.par.	300	Mark.par.		315	Mark.par.		173	Mark.par.		171
IdW	–	IdW		158	IdW		62	IdW		16
NW	307	NW		371	NW		374	NW		394

The crucifixion narrative of *Luke* can be seen even less than that of Matthew, purely as a work of redaction on the Marcan text. Luke knew Mark's narrative. But apart from his special material, which takes up more than half of his narrative (201 words of a total 374 words), there is also the sizeable portion (173 words) where his crucifixion narrative coincides with that of Mark, even though there are only sixty-two words which are identical in form and sequence. If one examines these verses, one finds in Luke 23.26, 33, 34b, 35c, 38, 44, 45b, 47, and 49 relatively frequent use of words which are identical in form and sequence. In some instances Luke renders Mark's verses more faithfully than does Matthew. Apart from this, Luke also has statements parallel to those of Mark in which there are no, or very few, words that are identical in form and sequence (cf. Luke 23.35d, 36, 46). Did Luke, in these verses, perform a more thorough redaction of Mark's version, or did he obtain similar material from a different source? And where did his voluminous special material come from?

Some scholars claim—in my view rightly—that apart from the Marcan text Luke in his redaction of the passion story also used another source. Whether he had available to him diverse traditions which he had collected, or one particular coherent source about the passion, cannot be established with certainty. It is equally difficult to determine whether Luke used the Marcan narrative as a foundation and added the special material to it, or whether he amplified the narrative of his special source by adding Mark's statements.

The fact that *John*, in his crucifixion narrative, follows a separate path while at the same time containing a surprising number of parallels with the synoptic Gospels, has already been noted. In his account of 394 words, a little less than two thirds is made up of special material (233 words). In the verses that are parallel to those of Mark, there are only sixteen words which are identical in form and sequence, and these never constitute a large percentage within their respective sentences. Therefore John, surely, did not merely amplify the Marcan account by use of special traditions. The coincidences with the synoptic traditions, however, are significant enough to show that John must have been familiar with them. For instance, he follows Mark and Matthew in their narrative structure for the way to the cross, crucifixion, division of garments, inscription of the cross, giving Jesus a drink, and death. Beyond that are congruities of idiom with Mark in John 19.17, 19, 24, 25 and 29; with Matthew in John 19.16, 17 (2 x), 19 (3 x), 29, and 30; with Luke in John 19.18 (2 x), 19, 25, 29, and 30. And finally, John, like Luke, omits the scene of Jesus being given wine and myrrh and the cry of Ps. 22.1 with the Elijah scene. Apart from the coincidences mentioned, John's crucifixion narrative shows too many particularities for it to be likely that he merely used the three synoptic accounts as models. It can be assumed with a greater degree of probability that John performed his work of redaction on a particular coherent oral or written source and that this source already contained links with the synoptic material.

This makes evident that it was not only Mark who gathered and transmitted pre-canonic crucifixion traditions. All four Evangelists, each in his own way, were transmitters and redactors of tradition. All of them were familar with the early Church's crucifixion traditions, but each had available to him separate collections of these pre-canonic narratives (cf. chapter 2, 2, especially the working hypothesis proposed in section 2 (i)). It is likely that all of them knew the early Church's credal formulae and songs, and perhaps even echoes of Pauline interpretations of these (cf. chapters 2, 3 and 3, 1–2). In the following four sections we shall examine how each of the Evangelists preached and taught anew the gospel of the crucifixion.

Some measure of circumambulation is unavoidable in this: our knowledge of the early Church's scriptural meditation and of pre-canonic crucifixion interpretation is derived from form-critical analysis and research into the history of the canonic narrative crucifixion tradition, and from the references to Scripture, pre-canonic credal formulae, and songs contained in the canonic New Testament. It is therefore not surprising that we find many elements of the early Church's theological work embedded in the canonic Gospels. In theory it is quite possible that the early Church's interpretations of the crucifixion were either forgotten or deliberately not passed on by the Evangelists. Traces of such interpretations might be present in the teachings of Paul's adversaries and in the non-canonic gospels. Research into the history of redaction must therefore not only be concerned with the sentences and additions potentially due to redaction. The selection made by individual Evangelists with regard to the traditions they used, and in particular with regard to their omissions, are theologically just as significant as their redactional additions.

2 The Crucifixion According to Mark

Who Mark was, for whom he wrote, and why, can only be guessed at. The narrator and the first readers of the 'Good News of Jesus Christ, the Son of God' have receded completely into the background. Based on sparse evidence contained in the Gospel and on doubtful information from the ancient church, it can be assumed that Mark was a gentile Christian and that he wrote his Gospel in the years A.D. 65–73, possibly for the Christian community in Rome.

It is possible that the community for whom he wrote, not unlike the one at Corinth, had emphasized Christ's resurrection and the spiritual presence of the risen Lord at the expense of Jesus, the man, and his way to the cross. This would explain why Mark wrote his Gospel in the first place, and why he stressed Jesus's way to the cross, the obscurity of the messianic king, and his passion, so strongly. It is also possible that at least some of the readers of the Gospel saw Jesus essentially as a man of miracles. Perhaps it was for this reason that Mark portrayed the disciples as those who did not understand the true being and the true mission of Christ, and who therefore had to learn that one can only perceive Jesus, the Son of God, by following him to the cross, and that thus it is possible to attain the right faith.

How Mark interpreted the crucifixion, however, cannot be deduced from such general assumptions about the origins of his Gospel. It is much more promising to examine his references to the Scriptures and his work of redaction on the crucifixion narrative.

i Mark's Reflection on Scripture

As the table of quotations and allusions to the Old Testament in chapter 2, 1 (ii) shows, the Evangelists in their crucifixion narrative refer to passages from the psalms of lament and praise, Pss. 22, 38, and 69. The early Church, because of the profound analogy of situation between the fate of Jesus and that of the psalmists, had come to the conclusion that Jesus was the suffering righteous one. Thus it had discovered the divine 'must' of the Messiah's passion. These key passages from the early Church's scriptural meditation were evidently so deeply rooted in the Church's tradition that they were even passed on by those bearers of tradition who did not interpret the crucifixion as a divine 'must', or see Jesus primarily as the suffering righteous one.

It is precisely the persistence of this traditional element, however, which allows us to discern that the Evangelists not only transmitted tradition, but also redacted it. They did not merely adopt the early Church's key texts about the significance of the crucifixion, but developed these traditions further, and thus reinterpreted the texts and the credal traditions that had been derived from them.

As shown in chapter 2, the early Church in its reflection on Scripture only rarely employed the conceptual pattern of prophecy/fulfilment. The earliest credal formulae contain no reference to Scripture and the earliest narrative passion tradition contained no reflective quotations. The passion was simply narrated in biblical language, that is to say, in the idiom of the Old Testament. This is also what Mark did, and in this he is closer to the early Church than the other Evangelists. He does not reflect upon prophecy and fulfilment, but recounts the scenes of the crucifixion in biblical language. As far as quotations from Scripture in his crucifixion narrative are concerned, he is much more a transmitter of tradition than a redactor.

ii Marcan Interpretations

The unprejudiced reader will observe that the passion story in the Gospel of Mark takes up a relatively large space. If one discounts the later addition (16.9ff) and the insertion of 15.28, the Gospel contains 660 verses, of which 103 belong to the passion story itself. If one considers that the passion story already begins with the entry into Jerusalem—which would be justified by the fact that Mark, significantly, then begins to give Jesus the title 'Lord'—it comprises no less than 217 verses, i.e. almost a third of the whole Gospel. Beyond that, there are many direct references to the passion in the first ten chapters (cf. 2.20; 3.6; 8.31; 9.12; 9.31; 10.33ff; 10.45). It is therefore not surprising that this Gospel has often been described as an extended passion story. In the passion according to Mark, the account of the crucifixion is of paramount importance. It has even been claimed to be the actual key to the comprehension of the entire Gospel. It is certainly true to say that the account of the crucifixion is the climax of the Marcan passion story. Mark transmits all three of the early Church's crucifixion traditions (cf. the working hypothesis proposed on pp. 43f above).

(1) Mark continued the *scriptural reflection*, which had begun shortly after Jesus's death, without significant modifications. He, too, by alluding to the psalms of lament, points to the divine 'must' of the repugnant events on the cross, to the Messiah's necessary death in order to transform our misery, and recognizes in him the suffering righteous one.

(2) The early Church's *eyewitness account* is not only passed on by Mark, but probably even amplified by redaction. The community for whom he wrote evidently knew the

sons of Simon Cyrene. For this reason, Mark—and only he—passes on their names, Alexander and Rufus (v. 21b). It was more likely theological-polemic purpose, rather than anecdotal interest, that led to this redactional addition. Mark probably wanted to show the community, who tended to overstress the miraculous and spiritual powers of the risen Lord, that 'this risen and now present Lord is the suffering Jesus of Nazareth, who calls us to follow him in his suffering. The man of miracles, empowered by the Spirit of the Lord, is the weak Jesus who broke down on the way to Golgotha and for whom Simon of Cyrene had to carry the cross. You all know the sons of Simon, who will bear me out.' It cannot be entirely ruled out that Mark, for this purpose, amalgamated the early Church's eyewitness account with interpretations derived from scriptural reflection and with prophetic-apocalyptic notions of Jesus's death. Be that as it may, Mark emphasized—by redactional addition or amplification of the eyewitness account—what happened at the crucifixion, and thus the agony of the crucified Jesus. The similarity between the Marcan and Pauline theology of the cross has rightly been observed, although it is impossible to prove any literary connection.

(3) The early Church's third interpretation, which saw Jesus's death as *cosmic judgement and historical turning point*, was also fully incorporated into Mark's Gospel. Only in his Gospel is the entire *schema* of three hours transmitted (Mark 15.25). In contrast to Matthew, however, he did not increase the number of apocalyptic signs. It might even be considered whether Matthew, with his many apocalyptic signs, preserved a tradition of the early Church, while Mark, by omitting the earthquake and the rising of the dead, made the events of the cross more 'historical'. Redactional addition must, however, be assumed for the scene describing the mocking of Christ (vv. 31–2a; possibly vv. 29c–32a). The two signs which Mark retained, and which he relates as having happened immediately before and after Jesus's death, point to judgement or new creation (the darkness in v. 33) and judgement on the temple (rending of the temple curtains in v. 38). But according to verses 31 and 32a, probably redactional, it is the priests who mock Jesus, and the Jewish

passers-by who echo Jesus's words about the temple. The catchwords are 'Come down!' 'Save yourself!'. But Jesus deliberately went *up* to Jerusalem. Obedient to God's will, he let himself be raised on the cross, since he did not want to save himself, but others (cf. Mark 10.45). All those who in their blindness cannot see this, who mock Christ and judge him, through the crucifixion are put under God's judgement. Moreover, even in their blindness they must still bear witness to Christ by expressing negatively what Jesus does positively by his dying: he destroys the temple (i.e. the meaning of worship in the temple of Jerusalem) and rebuilds it in three days (as the temple of the Holy Spirit, his community). What appears as Christ's exposure to insult and defeat is in fact his rise to victory and to glory.

Closely connected with the blind derision, there is a wish to 'see' a miracle, as Mark, and only he, relates: 'Let the Christ, the King of Israel, come down now from the cross, that we may see and believe!' (15.32a). In none of the other Gospels is Jesus portrayed so much a man of miracles as he is in Mark's. But now, at the decisive moment, Christ performs no miracle, nor does God save him by the miraculous intervention of Elijah. Mark's purpose was probably to redress the one-sided belief in Christ as the man of miracles, which was his evident intention throughout.

Those who have faith and seeing eyes, however, *can* see a miracle in the crucifixion: they can see a miraculous victory and a miraculous faith. This, at any rate, is what Mark endeavours to show his readers with his description of Jesus's death. A main theme of his Gospel is Jesus's fight with the powers of Satan. Consequently, the cry of death has occasionally been interpreted as a cry of victory. It has also been claimed that the Marcan crucifixion narrative constitutes a last and decisive account of exorcism: when Jesus drove out the evil spirits, he 'cried out with a loud voice' (1.26; 5.7). Jesus himself was seen by the scribes as one possessed (3.22; 3.30). This may also be behind the accusation of blasphemy (2.7; 14.64). In the eyes of the priests, Jesus was a man outside the law, an instrument of demonic powers, and the course of the crucifixion seemed to bear them out. Not the temple, but Jesus himself was now forsaken by God. But what does really happen? Does Mark describe Jesus's death as one last exorcism, whereby Jesus drove out the evil spiritis within him, as it were, at the cost of his own life? Yet the one who turns to God crying out in prayer does not fit the picture of a man possessed by demons, and the hypothesis of the crucifixion being a sort of exorcism is unconvincing. It is nevertheless clear that with Jesus's death something decisive and miraculous occurred, which Mark does not define closely but which he signifies with the end of the darkness and the rending of the temple curtains.

The first who saw 'that he thus breathed his last', that is to say, who not only heard the cry, but also noticed something of what was happening, was the Roman centurion. There is no doubt that the subsequent 'credo' constitutes a, or indeed *the*, climax of Mark's crucifixion narrative, irrespective of whether v. 39 should be considered traditional material or a redaction by Mark. How should this 'credo' be understood, though? It has frequently been pointed out that the title 'Son of God' is not only contained in the heading of the Gospel, but, apart from the stories of exorcism (3.11; 5.7), also appears at three crucial stages of Jesus's life: at his baptism (1.11), his transfiguration (9.7), and now at his death (15.39; cf. 14.61ff). This has given rise to the assumption that Mark wrote his Gospel as a liturgy of enthronement: at his baptism Jesus was adopted as God's Son, in his transfiguration he had appeared to his disciples in his glory as the Son, and in his death he was enthroned and publicly acclaimed the Son of God. In my opinion, this forces too schematic a structure upon the Gospel of Mark. It is, however, true to say that Mark in his passion story, and especially in his account of the crucifixion (vv. 26, 32), portrays Jesus as the messianic king, and this title of king is closely connected with that of 'Son of God'. But the main emphasis is not on enthronement, but on the paradox of the messianic king's forsakenness and suffering.

The centurion's 'confession of faith' has occasionally been interpreted in a missionary sense: indeed there are several passages in Mark's Gospel which indicate a connection between Christ's death and the coming world mission among the nations, e.g. the parable of the vineyard tenants

(12.1–12), and the anointing in Bethany (14.3–9). Only when Jesus's own people had rejected their Messiah, and after the judgement on the temple had been signalized, could the pagans be accepted. The centurion's credo would thus be the confessing Church's first harvest among the pagans. This is certainly true, but the question remains whether this missionary interpretation of the crucifixion is to be considered typical of Mark. The same might be said with equal justification of Matthew's crucifixion narrative, where not only the centurion but 'all that were with him' voice this belief.

One probably gets closest to Mark's theological intention if one understands the centurion's credo as follows: the high priests, the scribes, and, with them, all the people, were blind; they wanted to see a miracle and had therefore not recognized the essence of what was happening before their eyes. Nor did the disciples understand; they failed for a long time to recognize their master, and when they finally confessed that he was the Messiah, they misunderstood his way. They had not derided him at the crucial moment, but they had fled. One had betrayed his master, another had denied him. Jesus, the King of the Jews, was abandoned by his own people. The master, who had assembled the disciples and taught them the gospel, died alone, abandoned by them all. Even God seemed to have forsaken him, and in his recital of the psalm Jesus cried out for God's presence. Then, when the story of Jesus appears to have reached its ignominious end, the miracle happens: an outsider, a pagan, sees what has really occurred. He believes and confesses his belief. He does not remain alone, behind him are the women, who had followed Jesus already in Galilee and who 'came up with him to Jerusalem' (v. 41). To believe means to recognize the crucified one as the messianic king and Son of God. Therefore, in the Marcan crucifixion narrative, this first confessing Christian and the women are presented to the community afflicted by temptation as an encouragement and an example.

Jesus, the Messiah, is the suffering righteous one. Only as the one who was crucified can the risen Lord be known and recognized. The crucifixion constitutes judgement on the Jewish temple worship and the temple authorities, and in the agony on the cross the final decisive struggle with evil takes place. The account of the crucifixion thus becomes a call and an encouragement to faith, to follow Christ, and to bear his cross. All this Mark stressed, and all these accents, taken together, constitute the theological direction of his Gospel of the crucifixion.

3 The Crucifixion According to Matthew

Is the Gospel according to Matthew the writing of a single individual, perhaps a converted scribe, or is it the work of a whole school? Was the author (and possibly his school) a Jewish Christian who, in dispute with the synagogue, taught anew the tradition of Jesus, that had been passed on, to a strongly Hellenized mixed community of Jews and Gentiles? Or was he a gentile Christian who transmitted and interpreted the Jewish Jesus-tradition to a gentile Christian community? These questions are hotly disputed among present-day scholars.

A greater degree of unanimity exists in regard to the putative first readers. These were probably a Syrian community, possibly in a port on the Syrian-Phoenician coast, and the Gospel was most likely written in the period between A.D. 80 and 90. The original audience were evidently, like the disciples in the Gospel of Matthew, 'simple people' in search of greater righteousness. This community or brotherhood was troubled by 'false prophets', but these temptations were to be countered with this Gospel and its prophetic teachings which were linked strictly to Christ's commandments, enjoining a life dedicated to neighbourly love. What role did the Gospel of the crucifixion, and the new emphases derived from Matthew's scriptural meditation and redaction, play in this?

i Matthew's Reflection on Scripture

It is widely known that the Gospel of Matthew is based on intensive scriptural reflection. It contains many more quotations and allusions to the Old Testament than the other Gospels, i.e. about fifty-two quotations (compared with sixteen in Mark, eighteen in Luke and seventeen in John). If we include the allusions, there are about 146 direct and indirect references to the Old Testament (compared to seventy-one in Mark, 126 in Luke and twenty-three in John). Reflective quotations are particularly characteristic of the Gospel of Matthew. He and his school were convinced they possessed the true understanding of the 'law and prophets', for with Jesus Christ had appeared the one through whose teachings, deeds, and passion God's justice was fulfilled. In the Matthean community, therefore, the Scriptures were assiduously examined for those texts which had now been fulfilled through Christ. This intensive scriptural study is also recognizable in the Matthean crucifixion narrative, although less so than might be expected.

In the scene in which Christ is offered wine (v. 34), Matthew, in contrast to Mark, refers to Ps. 69.21 by saying, as in the Septuagint, that the wine was mixed with gall, instead of myrrh. He also employs the psalm's verbal form. In his description of the division of the garments (v. 35) Matthew also adapts his verbal form to the Septuagint version of Ps. 22.18. Perhaps this is just stylistic redaction, since Mark in his parallel text employs the historical present so typical of him. The 'wagging of heads', which recalls Psalm 22.7, is told by both Mark and Matthew in a form identical to that of the Septuagint text. Only Matthew adds in v. 43 to the mocking of priests, scribes, and elders an explicit quotation from Ps. 22.8. He largely follows the Hebrew text, but adds the word 'now'. Perhaps this is also intended as an allusion to Wis. 2.10ff. The fact that the cry of Ps. 22 (v. 46) had been transmitted in very different versions even in the traditions that were available to Mark and Matthew is shown by the many variants that exist in manuscripts and in the earliest traditions. Did Mark, whose predilection for the Aramaic idiom is also evident in other parts of his Gospel, aramaicize the Hebrew cry? Or, conversely, did Matthew translate the Aramaic cry into Hebrew in order to render the ensuing Elijah scene more comprehensible? If there is indeed factual historical recollection contained in the account of Jesus's cry of god-forsakenness, it would have to be established first in which language Jesus uttered it, and this is no longer possible. In connection with the sponge filled with

111

vinegar, Matthew (v. 48), just as Mark, refers to Ps. 69.21. In the psalm the drink meant torture. According to Mark and Matthew, however, this drink is intended to prolong Jesus's life, because the people want to see whether Elijah is going to intervene. Whether this is to be understood as a restorative or as mockery, however, does not become apparent.

In his crucifixion narrative, Matthew emphasizes the 'according to the Scriptures' more than Mark does. But in this, his work of redaction remains on quite 'traditional' lines. Matthew somewhat amplifies the implicit or explicit references to Scriptures contained in Mark and adds a quotation from oral tradition or his own reflection on Scripture (Ps. 22.8 in v. 43); yet it, too, is a quotation from the same Psalm 22 which had shaped the entire tradition. Matthew's crucifixion account contains no reference, either, to the servant of God who suffers for us. It is further worth noting that, despite the many references to Scriptures, there is no actual quotation of fulfilment. The reflective quotation contained in v. 35b, which was added to some of the old manuscripts, was probably transferred from John 19.24 by later copyists.

How can one explain this restraint in Matthew, whose scriptural meditation was otherwise so productive? One reason may be that, despite his frequent quotations from psalms, he does not accord them the same authority as he does the 'law and the prophets' and that therefore, for him, the psalms have no power of proof. Indeed, among Matthew's reflective quotations there is only one from a psalm (Matt. 13.35 = Ps. 78.2), and it is significant that it is prefaced as being the word of the prophet. This, however, serves only to explain the absence of references to psalms in Matthew's reflective quotations, but not his restraint in the use of scriptural meditation in his crucifixion account. He might, for instance, have quoted the to him well-known prophetic passage from Isa. 53, or a text from Exodus, Leviticus, or Deuteronomy which he frequently refers to elsewhere. Why did he not do this? Evidently the interpretation of Christ's death which pre-canonical reflection on Scripture had reached, fully accorded with his own theological view of the crucifixion. Therefore Matthew is content merely to make more explicit the references to psalms of lament and praise as transmitted by Mark. It is evident from his own references to Scripture in his crucifixion narrative that for him, too, Jesus is essentially the suffering righteous one, who was exalted by God. How Matthew, however, placed his specific accents in this traditional message can be gleaned from his redaction of the crucifixion narrative.

ii Matthean Interpretation

Most studies of Matthew's theology are based on the five-part structure of the main body of his Gospel (Matt. 3—25). They also point out that Jesus's teaching reaches its climax when the risen Christ, on the mountain of revelation, commands the Church to continue to teach and to make disciples of all nations (28.16–20). Research into the history of redaction, therefore, is remarkably unconcerned with the passion story, and the account of the crucifixion in particular. The passion is taken as an epilogue to the main body of the work, or at most as a stage on the way to enthronement.

Even special studies of Matthew's passion story are based to only a somewhat limited degree on his redaction of the crucifixion narrative. In these studies the accent is on Christ's majesty in his passion: Jesus might ask the Father for more than twelve legions of angels (26.53). He has the power to destroy the temple of God and to rebuild it in three days (26.61; cf. difference from Mark 14.58). As in John's Gospel, so also according to Matthew Jesus knows when his hour is come (Matt. 26.18). He knows his betrayer and even asks him to do his work (26.50), just as from the beginning of the passion he knew of his delivery to the cross (26.2). This knowledge does not lead him into despair but to his majestic answer to the questions by the high priests, couched in terms of a Christian creed (Matt. 26.63ff). Thus, words and signs from the sovereign Lord are to be found throughout Matthew's passion story. In many ways, therefore, Matthew prepares the way for John's interpretation of the crucifixion.

The question is whether this does not put too much emphasis on Christ's majesty in his crucifixion. It is true that three times in this crucifixion narrative Jesus appears as the

Son of God. He is addressed as such in mockery (vv. 40 and 43b), and confessed as such by the centurion and his soldiers (v. 54). According to Matthew, it is not at his resurrection that Jesus is enthroned as the Son of God and King. He is the Son from the beginning and remains so even during crucifixion. Matthew underlines this with his reference to Ps. 22.8 in v. 43 which appears in his Gospel only.

Those who merely emphasize that even on the cross Jesus remains the Son of God, misunderstand Matthew's Gospel of the crucifixion. The significant point here is that the Son of God, with all his power and authority, does not use his power but becomes god-forsaken. Matthew passes on the many references to the suffering righteous one, not merely because he wishes to be faithful to the tradition, but also because it is crucial for his testimony of Christ to contrast the majesty of Jesus with his god-forsakenness, his authority as the Son of God with his helplessness in death. His description of the crucifixion closely echoes the story of the temptation of Christ: 'If you are the Son of God, throw yourself down' (4.6). 'Save yourself! If you are the Son of God, come down from the cross' (27.40). Perhaps Matthew wished to recall the temptation by describing Jesus's rejection of the wine and his renunciation of his power. That Jesus is the Son of God is demonstrated by his resisting temptation and thus proving himself as God's righteous one. Already during his struggling prayer in Gethsemane, Jesus had repeated literally a plea from the Lord's Prayer (this only according to Matthew): 'Thy will be done' (26.42). Now, on the cross, Jesus also trusts in God, as witness the Jewish elders by their mockery. Even in his moment of god-forsaknness, he prays to God and obeys his will.

As Jesus is the Son of God in this way, with his death theophany occurs, God's presence is made manifest through signs. The earthquake and the other occurrences connected with it (related only by Matthew, vv. 51b–3) ought probably to be seen as such. These signs are, as a rule, interpreted as omens of the last day, and as such they were certainly meant when the early Church interpreted Jesus's death as judgement and turning point. It has been claimed that Matthew went a step further, and interpreted Jesus's death as the beginning of the return of the Son of God and as the coming of the Kingdom of God. According to this theory, it was Matthew who continued the cosmic-apocalyptic interpretation of Christ's death most consistently (cf. chapter 2, 2 (iii)). It appears to me, however, that the Matthean crucifixion narrative links the events following Jesus's death less with the end of the world than with resurrection (v. 53) and incipient world mission (v. 54). In the Old Testament such signs as earthquakes, in particular, but also the splitting of rocks and the opening of tombs, are considered not only as omens of the last day, but as indications of theophany. It is not advisable, though, to make too strict a distinction between theophany and the last day, especially as the raising of the dead is also recorded. If one examines the earthquake-motif in the Gospel of Matthew, the following conclusions can be drawn: in Matthew's apocalyptic description, taken over from Mark 13.8, the earthquake is probably meant as a sign of Christ's return and of the end of the world (cf. Matthew 24.3). In all other passages, though, the earthquake is a sign of God's presence: 8.24; 21.10; 28.2; 28.4 (these verses all stem either from Matthew's special material or from his redaction). The earthquake at Christ's death (27.51; 27.54) ought surely to be interpreted in this sense.

Graeco-Roman civilization knew of instances when on the death of illustrious people darkness, earthquakes, splitting rocks, and opened tombs were seen. The signs observed at Christ's death, though, should not be equated with this sort of parallel from religious history, but should rather be seen in the context of Old Testament and intertestamental texts about theophany. Psalm 18 is particularly closely related to Matthew's crucifixion narrative and also shows a remarkable number of parallels with Ps. 22. It is therefore quite possible that Matthew also had this psalm and similar passages from Scripture in mind when writing his narrative, even though he made neither direct nor indirect reference to Scripture.

With God being present in his Son, who is obedient to the last, world mission begins. The centurion and the soldiers, who had mocked him only a few hours earlier (27.27–31), recognize that Jesus is the Son of God. This might be translated as 'a Son of God', i.e. an extraordinary human being, and if the centurion indeed made this statement, as related by Mark and Matthew, he probably meant no more than that. It is known that imperial inscriptions of the first century sometimes used this title. In the Gospel of Matthew, however, this statement has a completely different implication, it is an unheard-of challenge to both Jewish and Graeco-Roman 'faith'. Therefore, to remain true to Matthew's intention, this statement must be translated with its full theological weight as '*the* Son of God'.

The theophany at Christ's death, and the world mission which this starts, brings a turning point in the history of salvation and, with it, judgement on the leaders of the people of Israel and on the Israelites whom they had led astray. It is no accident that, according to Matthew, the entire leadership was assembled around the cross; not only high priests and scribes, as in Mark 15.31, but the elders as well (Matt. 27.41). In contrast to Mark, Matthew restricted the mission of the mortal Jesus to the people of Israel (Matt. 10.5–6). Now the high priests and the entire council have passed judgement on Israel's Messiah, based on the evidence of false witnesses: 'He deserves death' (26.57, 59, 65ff). Despite the 'pious' premonition of a pagan woman (27.19), and against Pilate's will (27.24), the people, who have been led astray by their leaders, shout 'Let him be crucified' (27.20, 22, 23), and have thus taken the responsibility for Jesus's death sentence upon themselves (27.25). This delusion reaches its dramatic climax during crucifixion (mockery) and death (rending of the temple curtain). For Matthew, who in this is similar to John, all members of the people of Israel are henceforth 'the Jews'. (Matthew uses this term for the first time in 28.15, i.e. *after* the crucifixion.) One period in the history of salvation has come to an end and the period of world mission has begun. It would be incorrect, however, to speak so soon about the 'end of Israel' and 'the new Israel' (concepts unknown to Matthew and indeed non-existent in the New Testament). The saints who have been raised from their tombs are probably the faithful Israelites of the Old Testament. The eleven disciples, too, who first receive the command of world mission, are members of this people. Matthew writes neither for Jewish nor Gentile Christians, but, as the conclusion of his Gospel makes clear, for a 'universal Christian Church'.

According to Matthew, the passion, and especially the crucifixion, is neither an epilogue nor a phase on the way to enthronement, but the very core of his Gospel. Although Matthew transmits many of the early Church's interpretations—and in this he is close to Mark—his Gospel also contains new and quite specific emphases. Jesus on the cross proves himself as the righteous one and the Son of God, precisely because he withstands temptation and trusts in God even in his god-forsakenness, and is obedient to God's will to the last. For this reason, God has raised his Son. At Jesus's death and resurrection theophany occurs, a turning point in the history of salvation, the beginning of world mission. For the afflicted community of 'simple people' this interpretation of the crucifixion was at one and the same time a message of hope and an admonition to perseverance.

4   The Crucifixion According to Luke

In contrast to the other Evangelists, Luke begins the narrative of his Gospel by writing in the first person singular and directly addressing his first reader—or at least the person to whom he dedicates his book. In his case it appears at first glance possible, after all, to determine the *Sitz im Leben* of the Lucan account through its author and its original audience, and thus also to understand his crucifixion narrative in the light of this knowledge. The introductions to the Gospel and the Acts of the Apostles, however, simply follow the pattern and the style of the authors of antiquity. Therefore, we can at most guess about the person of Theophilus, who is mentioned both in Luke 1.3 and Acts 1.1, and it is equally impossible to glean much information about Luke or his Gospel's *Sitz im Leben*. The Gospel's inherent evidence appears to indicate that Luke was a gentile Christian and wrote for gentile Christians, at roughly the same time as Matthew. In the manner of a classical writer, he collected the traditions about Jesus which he had obtained from Mark and other sources, and reinterpreted them as a story of salvation. In contrast to the other evangelists, Luke wrote a Gospel in two parts: volume 1, containing the words and deeds of Jesus, the man, on his way from Galilee to Jerusalem, and volume 2, about the words and deeds of Jesus, the risen Christ, whose way leads from Jerusalem to the ecumenical community.

Nowhere is the situation of Theophilus, or that of the community for whom Luke wrote, expressly discussed. From the descriptions in both volumes of the situation the disciples and the first communities found themselves in, it is possible, however, to draw conclusions as to the original readers. It gives a picture of a fluctuating crisis situation, where the word of God always regains supremacy, however afflicted, vulnerable, or hopeless the community's position may appear. Persecution is frequently mentioned, as is dissension within the brotherhood. One may therefore deduce that Luke wrote with predominantly pastoral intent for a community that had begun to be discouraged by afflictions both from without and within.

i *Luke's Reflection on Scripture*

According to Luke 24.26ff, 44ff it was the risen Jesus himself who gave the impetus for early Christian scriptural meditation about the meaning of his death: 'That everything written about me in the law of Moses and the prophets and the psalms must be fulfilled.' And after Jesus had opened the disciples' minds to the understanding of Scripture, he expressly said: 'Thus it was written, that the Christ should suffer and on the third day rise from the dead and that repentance and forgiveness of sins should be preached in his name to all nations, beginning from Jerusalem' (24.44ff). These verses contain no less than four of Luke's favourite words. Luke not only transmitted the early Church's claim that Christ had to suffer 'according to Scripture', but also strongly emphasized that point himself, and throughout his Gospel he continued the early Church's reflection on Scripture and from it interpreted the death of Jesus anew.

Luke's references to Scripture cannot be subsumed under a single heading. He frequently tells the story of salvation by allusions to the Old Testament, without bringing the pattern of prophecy/fulfilment into play. Specific quotations often have the function of invoking Scripture as proof, without however presenting any reflections on whether what had been prophesied earlier has now been fulfilled. But alongside this, there exist specific quotations where texts of the Old Testament are cited as prophesying events in the life of Jesus, or where, based on such Old Testament passages, events are signalled as being their fulfilment.

Luke, too, in his crucifixion narrative is predominantly a transmitter of tradition. He freely incorporates the early Church's key texts into his narrative, as for instance the division of the garments (v. 34b), but, compared with Mark and Matthew, his references to Scripture are stressed either less (as in v. 36, vinegar) or more (as in v. 49, distant onlookers). Luke also replaces some of the early Church's key texts by other, similar ones, also from the psalms of lament and praise. The passers-by of Ps. 22.7b who wag their heads, in Luke's v. 35 are replaced by all who 'see' and 'mock' from Ps. 22.7a (but Luke divides them into the people who watch and the leaders who mock). Even more remarkable is the substitution, for Mark's and Matthew's cry from Ps. 22.1, of the prayer of faith of Ps. 31.5 in the Lucan account of Jesus's death. Did Luke here use special traditional material regarding Jesus's last words, or did he transform the tradition passed on by Mark? Either is possible. If it was a special tradition according to which Jesus in his death recited the Jewish evening prayer, Luke may have preferred this version to the Marcan tradition. Or Luke may have transformed Mark's tradition because he misinterpreted the cry of Ps. 22.1 as one of despair—or feared his Greek readers might misunderstand it as such—and therefore replaced this offending cry by the word of faith from another psalm of lament.

Among Luke's special material there appears in v. 30 explicit reference to Hos. 10.8. In contrast to, say, Luke 4.16–21, where a prophetic statement is described as having been fulfilled 'today', the quotation from Hosea is a pointer to a prophecy that still remains to be fulfilled (v. 30). What happens at the crucifixion is not yet the last judgement. But the pointer to the coming judgement makes clear that with Jesus's death something is happening that is closely connected with the last day.

Luke's special material is much more strongly influenced by another passage from Scripture—Isa. 53.12c—yet the reference to this passage does not appear in the crucifixion narrative, but already in 22.37, from which point he later enters into the Marcan crucifixion narrative (Mark 15.28): 'For I tell you that this Scripture must be fulfilled in me, "And he was reckoned with the transgressors".' This is the only clear reference to Isa. 53 in the passion stories of all four Gospels. It appears in a context, and with a preface, that leads one to assume it a Lucan redaction. According to this statement by Luke, Jesus identified himself with the suffering servant of the Lord. It is significant, though, that Luke does not quote Isa. 53.4–12b, but v. 12c, that is to say that part of the verse which, in contrast to v. 12b and 12d, is not about redemptive suffering. This strictly limited quotation of fulfilment from Isa. 53 has strongly influenced Luke's crucifixion narrative. In contrast to the other Evangelists, Luke mentions the transgressors already on the way to the cross: 'two others, also, who were criminals, were led away to be put to death with him' (v. 32). Jesus is thus reckoned among the transgressors. As they are crucified, so is he. Again in contrast to Mark and Matthew, Luke writes in one and the same sentence: 'They crucified him and the criminals' (v. 33). Only Luke mentions for a third time the two who are crucified with Jesus, in v. 39, using the same verb 'hang' that he later used twice in Acts for the crucifixion of Jesus (Acts 5.30; 10.39). Jesus is 'under the same sentence' as the criminals (v. 40), but he is innocent, as one of the criminals avows (v. 41). Therefore, God will frustrate this human sentence with his plan of salvation (Acts 3.14ff), and the prophecy of Isa. 53.12c is now fulfilled: Jesus is the suffering righteous one who has been 'reckoned among the transgressors.' Those who recognize and believe this can be saved (vv. 42–3). In this sense—and in this only—can it be said that the soteriological significance of Jesus's death in Luke's crucifixion narrative was derived from Isa. 53.

ii *Lucan Interpretation*

In Mark's Gospel the crucifixion is in many ways both the climax and the decisive conclusion of his account. Matthew links Jesus' death closely with his resurrection, and these two events, taken together, constitute a deep hiatus in the story of salvation. Luke, however, continues his narrative beyond the crucifixion without a break, and goes on to relate what the risen Christ after three days had said and done on earth. According to his account, the true turning point in the story is Christ's ascension, which he relates twice (Luke 24.51ff; Acts 1.9ff), each time from a different standpoint.

The ascension is of course closely connected with Christ's resurrection and the pentecostal experience. In Luke's theological thinking, Jesus's death seems thus to have less importance. It appears only as an intermediate stage on the way to resurrection. Salvation does not appear to be linked with his death, but with his resurrection and rise to glory.

It has therefore often been maintained that, according to Luke, Christ's death had little significance, or at least none for salvation, and that Luke described the passion purely as the martyrdom of the righteous one, and thus replaced the theology of the cross by a theology of exaltation. In view of the overall concept of Luke's two volumes, and of many individual passages, this claim might indeed be considered justified.

However, there also exist many other passages, particularly verses that have their origin in special material or redaction, which would contradict this claim. This can be demonstrated by two examples: (1) the 'here and now' of salvation in Luke's Gospel, and (2) Luke's emphasis on Christ's passion.

(1) According to Luke the Spirit does not first become effective with the event of Pentecost, but is already present and effective in Jesus, the man (Luke 4.1, 14, 18). Therefore the prophecies of salvation in the Old Testament are not fulfilled only with the resurrection, ascension, and the gift of the tongues, but 'today' (4.21; cf. further special material in 2.11; 13.32; 19.5,9), i.e. when Jesus, in the power of the Spirit, begins to preach in Nazareth, after the devil has left him 'until an opportune time' (4.13). The opportune time is the passion, when, according to Luke, Jesus is again tempted by the devil and resists this last temptation through the power of the Spirit. Thus, according to Luke, just as in Mark, the

passion is a decisive struggle. In the midst of this struggle—and not only after the resurrection—the 'here and now' of salvation is stated again: one of the robbers asks Jesus to remember him on the day of judgement. But Jesus replies: '*Today* you will be with me in paradise' (23.43). With this sentence Jesus not only combines Jewish apocalyptic concepts of salvation (paradise) with the existential experience of salvation (to be in Christ), but also responds to the expectation of future salvation, with salvation that is experienced this day. Although Luke writes his Gospel as a story of salvation, he does not think of time as a progression according to the calendar, which leads from one epoch to the next. For him, too, a new time has begun with the advent of Jesus, though it still overlaps with the old time. Salvation, therefore, is not exclusively linked with the resurrection of Christ, but with the entire Jesus event. This includes his miraculous birth, his sermons, his acts of power, his endurance in suffering, and his death, just as much as his resurrection, ascension, the gift of the Spirit, and his return.

(2) It is not intended here to deny that in both Luke's works the main accent is on Christ's ascension. From the wealth of the early Church's credal formulae Luke tended to select those of resurrection in preference to those of God giving his Son or of Christ's death. It is nevertheless remarkable to observe how expressly Luke describes Jesus's life as the path of the suffering Christ. From the stories of his infancy to his death and thence to the risen Lord's instruction and the sermons in Acts, the necessity of the passion is emphasized again and again. Luke not only transmitted the early Church's traditions about the divine 'must' of the passion, as did Mark and Matthew, but he made this tradition the central theme of his passion story. In the Lucan crucifixion story particularly, Jesus appears primarily as the innocent sufferer who goes the way ordained by God, and who even in death remains steadfast in his faith in God (23.46). As such he is the suffering righteous one. One of the criminals even voices this during the crucifixion (v. 41), and immediately after Jesus's death the centurion praises God and confesses: 'Certainly this man was innocent' (v. 47). In this account the intention is surely not to point to Jesus's inno-

cence for reasons of apologia, but, in line with the early
Church's interpretation of the cross, to confess here that
Jesus was the innocently suffering *righteous* one. It was Luke
who applied Isa. 53.12 to Jesus in this way and also he who,
in Acts 3.14; 7.52; 22.14, described Jesus as the righteous
one.

In his redaction of the crucifixion narrative, Luke does
however go beyond the early Church's interpretation of
Jesus's death as a divine 'must'. He does not do so by
employing the concept of vicarious redemption, nor by
interpreting the death as one of atonement and sacrifice.
Nowhere in his two works does he say that Jesus died 'for our
sins' or 'for the many'. True, he was familiar with the early
Church's interpretation, and transmitted it in somewhat
modified form in his preface to the last supper (Luke
22.19–20; 'poured out for you') and in Paul's valedictory
words to the elders of the community at Ephesus ('which he
(God) obtained with the blood of his own son', Acts 20.28).
However, Luke does not stress this interpretation and, like
Mark and Matthew, omits it from his crucifixion narrative.
This has led to the claim that, according to Luke, Jesus's
death possesses no significance for salvation. It is true that
Luke does not stress the concept of the redeeming death, but
it has already been demonstrated that in his Gospel Jesus's
death is linked indivisibly with his resurrection and thus with
salvation.

The special material about the crucifixion contained in
Luke's Gospel confirms this. The presence of the populace
and the many women is typical (23.27, 35, 48), and these are
not derisive bystanders, but witnesses to the event. What do
they see and hear? Even on the way to Golgotha, Jesus
already refers to the coming judgement (vv. 28–30). The fire
of judgement is paradoxically ignited on the green and not on
the dry wood, that is to say on Jesus, in whose passion and
death judgement has already begun (thus the difficult verse
31 might well be understood). In the face of the coming
judgement there is, however, one way to salvation—to
follow Christ. Luke demonstrates this in his redactional
modification of the tradition about Simon of Cyrene (v. 26):
he was 'seized' to carry the cross 'behind Jesus'. For Luke,

Simon is thus not predominantly a witness of the crucifixion, but the example of a disciple who has taken seriously Jesus's word about taking up his cross (Luke 9.23). Jesus goes ahead. Whoever mocks him will meet with disaster, be they the Jewish authorities, soldiers, or a criminal. This may be the reason for Luke's placing the time of the rending of the temple curtain and the darkness before Jesus's death (vv. 44ff). Whoever remains with Jesus, though, may have trust even in the face of judgement (vv. 41ff), for Jesus is not only the innocently suffering righteous one, the example to the Church of the martyrs, but also the one who has authority to absolve from sin (v. 34). This power of forgiveness creates the miracle of conversion. For Luke, therefore, the signs which accompany Jesus's death are not primarily cosmic-apocalyptic occurrences, but changes that take place in the hearts of men: one of the criminals silences the chorus of mockers (vv. 41ff), and the attendant representative of the Roman legislature declares that Jesus died as an innocent (v. 47). The multitude is moved to repentance (v. 48).

By accentuating these points in his crucifixion narrative, Luke proclaims Jesus's death as gospel to an afflicted and persecuted community. Like Paul, Mark, and Matthew, Luke in his own way is both a transmitter of tradition and at the same time an independent interpreter of the message of the cross.

5 The Crucifixion According to John

The Gospel of John is probably the boldest new interpretation of the gospel traditions. In an addendum to this work (John 21), the anonymous favourite disciple is indicated as the author. The author himself is intent on preserving his incognito, and does not divulge which community he is addressing in order to strengthen its faith. As with the other Gospels, the hypotheses with regard to its *Sitz im Leben* can only be based on its internal evidence and on sparse points from the church Fathers. It is usually assumed that the redaction of the Gospel of John, as we know it, was carried out in Asia Minor between A.D. 90 and 100. Yet this redaction bears clear traces of the existence of an older history, and an earlier *Sitz im Leben* may have been in Judaea or, more likely, Syria.

With what purpose did this Gospel come to be written? It is unlikely to have been intended for the conversion of Jews in the diaspora, as is occasionally contended. The choice of central concepts in this Gospel points in quite another direction. Was it the intention to reinterpret the Gospel tradition as a myth of redemption, in order to counter the concepts of gnostic philosophy? This would mean that Jesus is interpreted as the Revealer who had come from heaven and returned to heaven. Yet the arguments in the Gospel of John are not merely aimed at another world of ideas, but against an entire world—primarily the Jewish world—which hates and persecutes Jesus and his followers. Christians are excluded from the synagogues, they are accused, persecuted, dispersed, and many defect or, like the Apostle Thomas, begin to doubt. This was indeed the position of the Church in Asia Minor during the last decade of the first century A.D. It must therefore be assumed that the Gospel of John was written primarily for those Christians who were persecuted by both Jews and Roman legislators and who were troubled and discouraged in their faith. The writing of it, employing gnostic and Jewish sectarian concepts, led indeed to a new interpretation of the Gospel tradition. Yet the author is unlikely to have intended to correct wrong faith or to devise a new theology. The purpose of this Gospel was rather to encourage the faith of its readers by giving them also a theological understanding of their situation as a persecuted people. Which were the aspects John emphasized through scriptural meditation and redaction of the Gospel tradition?

i   *John's Reflection on Scripture*

John's crucifixion narrative contains many fewer references to the Old Testament than do the synoptic accounts. Does this mean he did not continue the early Church's reflection on Scripture? John tended to turn individual scenes and statements contained in the synoptic Gospels into dimensions that informed his entire Gospel. The most vivid example of this is the account of the transfiguration, which does not appear as such in his Gospel, but as a dimension dominates it throughout. It is likely that John proceeded in a similar manner with the texts from the Old Testament. He does not use individual passages from the Old Testament as scriptural proof, but instead takes the Old Testament as a whole, or at least its themes and images. In doing so, he does occasionally quote Old Testament texts, but more as an example or model for an entire train of thought. It is therefore often difficult to establish which Old Testament passage is being referred to. John 19.36, with its echoes of Exod. 12.46, Num. 9.12, and Ps. 34.20, is a typical example.

John's reflection on Scripture, in the main, refers to the same books of the Old Testament as the Synoptics, i.e. the prophets and the Psalms. Formally, in his use of Scripture, John is closest to Matthew, for the latter, too, gives several quotations of fulfilment. Whereas in the Matthean crucifixion story these are of relatively minor importance, in John's crucifixion narrative formulae of fulfilment appear in great number. Twice they refer to Jesus's own words (John 18.9, 32), while of the eight or nine quotations from Scripture in John's passion text, six are prefaced with a formula of fulfilment (John 13.18; 15.25; 19.24; 19.28; 19.36; 19.37). Four of these are contained in the crucifixion narrative, which thus, like the other Gospels, bears a clear imprint of the Old Testament.

In contrast to the Synoptics, allusive references to Scripture are not much in evidence in John's Gospel. A clear case of this is John 19.23ff. The story of the division of the garments and the casting of lots for the seamless robe is at first told without any scriptural allusions and without any of John's linguistic idiosyncrasies. Psalm 22.18 is cited only afterwards, and that in an exact quotation from the Septuagint text and with a preface typical of John: 'This was to fulfil the Scripture.' John has turned the early Church's *references* to Scripture into *proof* by Scripture. According to him, the details of the crucifixion are not left to the whims of man, but are ordained by God. John is alone in relating the drawing of lots for the seamless garment. Whether this scene has been invented, based on a no longer intelligible parallel with Psalm 22.18, or whether it constitutes factual recollection only available to John, can no longer be established. It is moreover worth considering whether John took the double statement contained in Ps. 22.18 literally because the seamless robe had symbolic significance for him. Some exegetes interpret the passage therefore as follows: Jesus, the true high priest, is robbed of his priestly garment at the very moment when he offers himself up as sacrifice. Many statements in the Gospel of John have indeed a double significance: first he tells a concrete event in Christ's life—here the division of his garments and its accordance with Scripture—and at the same time he points to a meta-historical reality, in this case possibly the paradox of Christ's performing also the service of high priest.

A similar double meaning can be observed in other scriptural proofs quoted in John's crucifixion narrative. In the passage describing the drink of vinegar, John with his reference to Ps. 69.21b and 19.28ff adds certain important features which point beyond the narrated event to a meta-historical significance. Here are three examples: (1) Jesus says 'I thirst'. Whether this is a reference to Ps. 69.21b or to Ps. 22.15, or both, remains uncertain. Jesus's thirst is probably mentioned in the first place to emphasize that he is human, that he has become flesh (John 1.14a); but beyond that it points to the paradox that one who has in his giving the eternally thirst-quenching water of life, should now be thirsty. (2) The sponge with vinegar, according to John, is not given to Jesus on a 'reed' (as in Mark and Matthew), but on 'hyssop'. Hyssop, according to Lev. 14.4, 6, 49–52, was used in the Jewish cleansing rituals. It is thus possible that John, like Paul in 1 Cor. 5.7ff, interprets Jesus's death as a Christian feast of Passover. The imagery, however, is not clear, and 'hyssop' might equally have been mistaken for the similar sounding Greek word for 'spear'. (3) The last quotation from Scripture before Jesus's death is not prefaced by the usual formula of fulfilment. John writes instead: 'Jesus, knowing that all was now finished, said (to fulfil the Scripture) . . .' John usually uses the verb 'finish' in connection with the 'work' of the Father. And now, with his death, Jesus finishes his Father's work of salvation. The last phase of this work, and thus Jesus's death, is announced as the accomplishing of Scripture and of God's will revealed therein.

The last two references to scriptural proof in John's crucifixion story (19.36ff)—also the last in his Gospel—have no synoptic parallels. As in vv. 23ff, the events are related first: in this case that Jesus's legs are not broken and that his side is pierced with a spear. The double quotation of fulfilment is only added afterwards. The first quotation follows neither the exact wording of Exod. 12.46 or Num. 9.12 nor of Ps. 34.20. It is impossible to deduce from the text of the quotation which of these passages John is referring to, if indeed he is not alluding to several Old Testament texts. An interpretation of this quotation from Scripture can therefore only be attempted in the light of John's overall interpretation of the crucifixion.

Those who assume that John interpreted Christ's death in the sense of the slaughter of a Passover lamb, will prefer the reference to Exod. 12.46 and Num. 9.12, because it is written there that the bones must not be broken. This would make the date of death, which differs from that given by the synoptic Gospels, theologically significant. According to John, Jesus was crucified on the eve of Passover, at about the same time that Passover lambs were slaughtered in Jerusalem. What the feast of Passover means to the Jews, for the faithful Christians would be Jesus's crucifixion: he is the true Passover lamb. He dies on the cross to save the world. This interpretation, however, has only a narrow base in John's Gospel. The 'Lamb of God' in John 1.29, 36, which is usually cited in corroboration, is not described as a Passover lamb. According to Exod. 12 it would have no power of redemption anyway. By Lamb of God John might equally have meant a sacrifical lamb, the lamb of Isa. 53, or the sin offering for the great ritual of Atonement (Lev. 16). Even the link between the hyssop mentioned in 19.29 and the Passover ritual remains doubtful. It is significant that the Passover lamb plays no part at all in the very passages where John specifically writes about the soteriological meaning of Jesus's death (cf. 3.14–16; 10.11, 15; 11.50–2). It is also worth noting that, according to John, Jesus never said: 'I am the Passover lamb,' although elsewhere, in connection with Jewish feasts, he did employ such interpretative descriptions of himself.

Those who are of the opinion that John, in his reference to scriptural proof texts, is mainly transmitting early Church traditions, will regard the quotation in 19.36b rather as a reference to Ps. 34.20. This proclaims, entirely in line with other early Church references to psalms of lament and praise, that God preserves and saves the suffering righteous. In this context it might mean preservation for the resurrection, since according to (later?) Jewish belief, mutilation of the corpse might constitute an impediment to resurrection. It would, however, be difficult to explain why John in this particular instance transmitted early Church traditions. The purpose of the quotation is to corroborate a solemn eyewitness account—the only specific statement by an eyewitness in the entire Gospel—by reference to the authority of Scripture. John, with this last double quotation in his Gospel, evidently intended to make clear his specific interpretation of Christ's death.

Can the reference to Zech. 12.10, contained in v. 37, which is so closely linked to the quotation in v. 36, help to elucidate this point? Here we have a text which, at first glance, appears to be a prophecy of doom, yet at the same time promises the chosen people in the coming messianic time 'a spirit of compassion and supplication' which will lead to salvation (cf. Zech. 13.1). There are also echoes of Zech. 12.10 in Matt. 24.30, and we find this again in Rev. 1.7. In John's Gospel it is quoted in the context of Jesus being pierced by a spear. This piercing and the blood and water that flow from Jesus's side, followed immediately by the affirmation that an eyewitness had seen it, are probably intended mainly to stress Jesus's incarnation and the reality of his death. Some scholars take the view that this is its main, or even its only, significance. Yet it was surely John's intention to bear witness to more than the mere fact of Jesus's death, however necessary the affirmation of the reality of this death may have been in a gnostic environment. It is usually assumed that blood and water are a symbolic reference to Holy Communion and Baptism, or to the atoning power of the blood and the living water of the Spirit that flow from Jesus. Either is possible, and perhaps it was John's intention to indicate both: the power of salvation and Spirit emanating from Christ's death,

which immediately also brings to mind Communion and
Baptism. Where, however, is the link between this event and
the proof from Scripture, Zech. 12.10? As the purpose of the
Gospel throughout is to lead to faith (20.31), so is the story
of the piercing by a spear told and solemnly affirmed 'so that
you also may believe' (19.35b). The scriptural reference in v.
37 must probably be linked to the specific slant of what is
told in vv. 34ff. 'They shall look at him . . . so that they may
also believe.' Those who see are, in the first place the Roman
soldiers, and in the wider sense also the Jews (cf. 8.28). The
believers are primarily the members of John's community.
But those who see may also become believers. Seeing, to
them, at first means judgement. But if they 'see' in the specific
sense of the New Testament, that is, if they look up and
recognize the exalted Son of God in the crucified Jesus, they
receive salvation. What had been promised in Zech. 12.10 for
the time of the Messiah, can now become reality—not only
for the Israelites, but for all. It becomes reality through the
exaltation of Jesus on the cross and through his death of
salvation.

In my view, the main accent connected with the scriptural
proof from Zech. 12.10 is that Christ's death brings judgement and salvation to those who look up to the crucified one.
Does salvation come because Jesus dies as a Passover lamb,
or because he is exalted on the cross? Does John indicate
both? Probably the latter. The main emphasis of John's
interpretation of the crucifixion, however, is rather on salvation through the Father accomplishing his work of salvation
by exalting his Son on the cross, than on salvation through
the blood of the Passover lamb.

ii *John's Interpretation*

John does not spiritualize the events of the crucifixion. He
emphasizes the reality of Jesus's death even more than the
synoptic Gospels. He points more directly even than Mark to
the testimony of a credible eyewitness who was present at the
crucifixion. His first concern, like that of the other Evangelists, is to relate actual events and to ensure that belief is
anchored in history. Yet the Church was right in according to
the author of the fourth Gospel the title of 'theologian'. As

John narrates the story of the crucifixion, he lets his reader glimpse the deep inner meaning of outward events—to see meta-history in history, icons in his images.

In the testimony of John, Jesus's main characteristic is his being the sovereign Lord. In this, the fourth Evangelist adopted a theme from Mark's passion story and developed it much further. Christ's kingship is borne witness to by reversing roles and functions in an ironic manner: at his arrest, it is not Jesus and his disciples who are frightened, but the armed hordes who draw back and fall to the ground (18.6). In the trial scene the argument is about Jesus's kingship (18.33–40) and he is presented to the Jewish people as a king (19.4–5). Finally—although in a doubtful translation of 19.13—it is Jesus and not Pilate who sits on the judgement seat. Thus Jesus's adversaries are time and again turned into his intercessors, into unwilling witnesses to his kingship. On his way to the cross, too, Jesus goes ahead, and needs nobody to help him, for he is bearing his own cross. At the crucifixion Jesus is in the middle (v. 18). Despite the chief priests' protest, the tri-lingual inscription on the cross tells all the nations that this Jesus of Nazareth is King of the Jews. Many Jews read this (vv. 19ff), and the tri-lingual inscription may perhaps be taken as an ecumenical prophecy of Christ's kingship. To the last, Jesus is the one who acts (cf. 10.18). Even on the cross he looks after his own (vv. 26ff). Until the last moment he fulfils Scripture (vv. 28ff), and in death also the initiative is his: he dies amazingly quickly (v. 33). Some scholars claim that Jesus's bowing his head and giving up his spirit is further evidence of his own action (v. 30).

The royal character of the crucified Jesus is further emphasized by the absence of any mockery during his crucifixion. The two who are crucified with him are not described as robbers or criminals. According to John, Jesus is not as deserted by his followers as in the narratives of the synoptic Evangelists (despite 16.32a): his mother and other women, together with his loved disciple, do not look on from afar, but stand beneath the cross. Neither darkness nor other signs of judgement are mentioned, and Jesus dies, not with the cry of a psalm or a martyr's prayer, but declaring that now his Father's work is finished.

John, even more than Matthew, proclaims this crucified king as the Son of God. Indirectly, even the Jews and Pilate are made to testify to this in 19.7–9. In John's passion story there is no prayerful struggle in Gethsemane, for Jesus knows his Father's will. At one time he had feared the hour of his death (12.24–28a), but God gave him the promise: 'I have glorified it (my name), and I will glorify it again' (12.28b). This is the only passage in John's Gospel where God speaks directly. From this moment on, Jesus follows his path to the cross unperturbed. He speaks about his crucifixion and the meaning of what is happening (12.31ff). He knows that 'his hour' has come (13.1–3). He asks Judas Iscariot to accomplish his devil's work quickly (13.27), because he knows that thus God's work will be accomplished. Therefore he willingly leads the way to Gölgotha. Jesus's last word, 'it is finished', summarizes the whole of John's interpretation of his death: the work of the Father is accomplished, that is, the work of revealing love, of salvation. This last word must be read and understood in the context of statements such as those in 4.34; 17.4; 6, 37ff; 1.29; 3.14; 10.17ff.

It is also specific to John that the crucifixion is seen as exaltation (3.14; 8.28; 12.32, 34), and that there exists an inherent link between the raising up on the cross and the glorification of Father and Son. Most studies of John's passion story, therefore, interpret the crucifixion narrative wholly in the light of passages that proclaim his being raised up and glorified: Christ's execution was his enthronement, the cross became his throne, and the passion was the Revealer's triumphant return to heaven. This interpretation fits in well with John's whole conception of Christ. In the Gospel of John there exist, for instance, no specific annunciations of suffering, but there are three annunciations of the Son's return to the heavenly Father (7.32; 8,21; 13.33).

Those who see John's interpretation of the crucifixion purely as one of glorification overlook that John, too, had problems in fitting the repugnant event of the crucifixion into his theology. Significantly, in his crucifixion narrative, the verb 'raise' or the concept of exaltation do not appear. It should not be forgotten either that in central passages of John's passion story roles are *not* reversed. In his account, too, the homage to the king remains a scene of torture and mockery (19.1–3). The crown is a wreath of thorns (19.2); the robe of royal purple and his chief priest's garment (?) are taken from him; Jesus dies naked. He, who can give the water of life, thirsts. His throne is a cross—and both the fourth Evangelist and his original readers knew at first hand the stark reality of death by crucifixion.

How does the crucifixion relate to glorification? If even during Jesus's life on earth the glory of being God's Son was visible (1.14), if, even before the passion, Jesus was the resurrection and the life (11.25), what sense then was there in the passion?

Some scholars hold the view that the crucifixion had indeed posed a great problem for John, and that this is noticeable in his passion story. They say that the incorporation of early Church traditions into his Gospel added nothing new to John's interpretation of Christ, but served purely as a corrective to his dangerously one-sided theology of exaltation. It is indeed not impossible to mistake John's image of Christ for the one the enthusiastic Corinthians had formed. Had John omitted the passion, as did many authors of apocryphal gospels, his Gospel would not have been accepted into the canon. But John, too, became a transmitter of the passion tradition. Instead of writing a doctrine of salvation unconnected with the passion, he, too, bore witness to the fact that the heavenly Revealer was Jesus, who died on the cross.

The incorporation of the passion tradition into his Gospel certainly corrected John's theological thinking. It seems to me, though, that the crucifixion narrative in John's Gospel does not only fulfil this corrective function, but also demonstrates that it is precisely on the cross that the paradox of God's love is revealed. What is probably the most quoted Bible text about divine love (3.16) bears direct relation to a statement about the Son of God being exalted, which in turn points towards the crucifixion (3.14).

The work of the Father *must* be accomplished on the cross, for the greatest love is shown by laying down one's own life (15.13). It is this self-sacrificing love which constitutes the link between the raising up on the cross and the glory of

Father and Son. We have thus reached the core of John's message of the cross. The fourth Evangelist recognized the divine 'must' of the passion as a 'must' of love. He translated the early Church's credal formulae and songs of 'God giving his Son for us' into the passion story. One example of this love are the words the crucified one addresses to his mother and his favourite disciple (19.26–7). With a twofold formula of adoption he recommends his mother to the care of his favourite disciple. Mary and the women here represent the faithful community, and the favourite disciple is the true witness of Jesus, one might say the gospel of Jesus incarnate. Thus the deeper meaning of this scene is probably that Jesus refers the community to the message of the gospel and so ensures the unity of the Church.

Immediately after Jesus has given himself, it is solemnly affirmed that such love accomplishes the work of the Father: the piercing by a spear, intended to document his death, makes blood and water flow. This leads to the glory that brings salvation, to the message that creates faith, to the coming together of the community. From beneath the cross the persecuted and discouraged Christians of Asia Minor may look up to the king and recognize the Son of God in his glory. It is in the passion that the paradox of God's love is revealed.

Like the synoptic Evangelists, and Paul and the early Church before them, John was also a transmitter and interpreter of the crucifixion. The traditions and interpretations of all the authors of the New Testament have been incorporated in the canon of the Bible and accepted and preserved by the Church of all ages and continents as true and compelling testimony. The diversity within the unity of the canon also enables the Church of today, in quite new circumstances and environments, to bear witness to the crucified Jesus, to preach him and to follow him.

Descriptive Synopsis

The following synoptic comparison is based on the crucifixion narrative of Mark: the marginal note '20b Ev.' means that the statement contained in Mark 15.20b is common to all four Gospels. '21 Syn.' means that only Matthew and Luke contain a parallel statement to Mark. 'S' indicates special material, which is only found in one of the Evangelists. '23 Matt.' means that only Matthew has a parallel statement to. Mark's 15.23. Darts indicate differences in sequence: 'John ↑ ' = John brings this earlier than Mark; 'Luke ↓ ' = Luke makes this statement later than Mark; '(Luke ↓)' = indication of a parallel statement made later by Luke. Indented marginal signs indicate particularities within the scenes under discussion. All marginal notes are confined to the most important connections and divergences.

20b Ev.	The *way to the cross* is described only briefly by the Evangelists, mostly in just two sentences. In
Mark Matt.	contrast to Mark and Matthew, Luke and John have no final sentence 'to crucify him'. John writes
21 Syn.	nothing about *Simon of Cyrene*, since according to
Mark S	his statement Jesus bore the cross himself. Mark gives explanations about Simon which are left out completely by Matthew and partly by Luke. Only
Matt.	from Matthew's text might it be deduced that Jesus bore the cross himself, before it was given to Simon to carry. In addition, according to Matthew, Simon
Mark	was 'found' and not 'compelled' as Mark describes,
Luke	borrowing a Persian word. According to Luke, he is 'seized', not only to carry the cross, but to carry it
Luke S	'behind' Jesus. Luke 23.27–32 brings important spe-
Luke S	cial material about the '*great multitude of people*' and the *women*, as well as Jesus's word of admonition with a quotation from Hosea 10.8 and a remark about the criminals who were led away with him.
22 Ev.	According to all Evangelists the crucifixion took
Mark Matt.	place at *Golgotha*, but while Mark and Matthew

135

first give the Hebrew name and then translate it, Luke and John give only the translation, with John adding, however, that the place is called Golgotha in Hebrew. The *arrival at the place of execution* is related variously: according to Mark he is 'brought' to Golgotha, according to Matthew and Luke they 'came' to it (i.e. the soldiers, and according to Luke also the multitudes, with Jesus and the criminals); John relates only: 'He (Jesus) went out to the place called the place of the skull.' In Luke and John the crucifixion follows immediately. Mark and Matthew first relate the scene of Jesus being offered a *drink of wine* which he rejects after tasting it (Matthew). Mark says that it is wine spiced with myrrh; Matthew, in the sense of Ps. 69.21a, talks about wine mixed with gall. Mark and Matthew mention only *Jesus's crucifixion*, whereas Luke and John already describe the *crucifixion of the criminals*, one to the right and one to the left (Luke), or the 'crucifixion of two others, one on either side and Jesus between them' (John). Luke further adds *Jesus's word of forgiveness* although this is only dubiously attested in early manuscripts. The synoptic Evangelists then go on to describe the *division of the garments*, which John relates at a later stage. They do so using the words of Ps. 22.18 in its Septuagint version, with almost complete congruity between Mark and Matthew and only minor divergences in Luke. In some early manuscripts, Matt. 23.35 contains a reflective quotation from Ps. 22.18, probably taken over from John 19.24. Only Mark adds that it was the *third hour*, and only Matthew relates that the soldiers 'then sat down and kept watch over him there'. Mark, Matthew and John relate the *inscription on the cross*: according to Mark and Matthew (and also Luke who, however, tells this quite briefly later, in connection with the mocking) it is an 'inscription' (of the charge against him) which John describes by the word *titlos* borrowed from the Latin, and which also appears in apocryphal crucifixion narratives. The *inscription reads*: 'King of the Jews' (Mark); 'This is Jesus, the King of the Jews' (Matthew); 'This is the King of the Jews' (Luke); 'Jesus of Nazareth, the King of the Jews' (John). Regarding the *place of the inscription*, only Matthew and John relate that it was fastened on the cross, and only Matthew and Luke mention that it was 'over his head' (Matthew), or 'over him' (Luke). Only John

Marginal references:

- Luke John
- Mark
- Matt. Luke
- John
- (Luke John ↑)
- 23 Matt.
- Matt.
- 24a Ev.
- Luke ↑ John↑
- Luke
- Luke S   John
- 24b Syn.
- Luke
- Matt.
- 25 S
- Matt. S
- 26 Matt. John
- (Luke ↓)
- John
- Mark
- Matt. Luke
- John
- Matt. John
- Matt. Luke

John S relates that *Pilate* had written the inscription. In this
connection he adds further special material, with the
news that *many Jews read this* title, that it was
written in Hebrew, Latin, and Greek (some manu-
Luke scripts contain the same statement in Luke 23.38),
and that the inscription prompted a discussion between Pilate and the chief priests. Only now do Mark
27 Matt. and Matthew relate in almost identical form that
Jesus was crucified between *two robbers/rebels*
(Matthew might possibly be understood to mean that
they were crucified after Jesus). Only now does John
John ↓ describe in detail the division of the garments by the
John S soldiers, and he also mentions the *seamless robe* and
adds Ps. 22.18, as a reflective quotation.

In the section relating to events *around the cross*
John ↑ John and the synoptic Gospels differ most widely.
John S According to John 19.25–7, '*standing by the cross
were the women and the disciple whom Jesus loved*'
and into whose care he gives his mother. (The
synoptics only mention the women after Jesus's
death, and they look on from 'a distance'). According
Luke S to Luke, instead of the women '*the multitudes*' stood
and looked on. According to the quite identical
29ff Matt. statements in Mark and Matthew *those who passed
by* derided him, 'wagging their heads' (quotation
from Ps. 22.7b). Only Mark and Matthew also state
what the mockers said: reiterating Jesus's word
about the temple and calling on him to save himself
and to come down from the cross. Apart from
Matt. S Matthew's addition 'if you are the Son of God', both
Evangelists employ identical concepts. The ensuing
31ff Syn. similar *mocking by chief priests, scribes* (and *elders*,
Matthew), or more generally, by the *rulers* (Luke), is
mentioned by the three synoptics, each however uses
Mark a different *title*: 'The Christ, the King of Israel'
Matt. (Mark); 'the King of Israel' (Matthew); 'the Christ of
Luke God, his Chosen One' (Luke). Only Mark mentions
Mark S that the scoffers wanted to 'see' in order to believe,
Matt. S while only Matthew added the quotation about trust
in God from Ps. 22.8, and a renewed pointer to the
fact that Jesus had called himself the Son of God.
Luke S Only Luke relates the *mocking by the soldiers*, which
Luke ↑↓ he links with his earlier mention of the drink of
vinegar and the inscription which he mentions only
at this stage (Mark and Matthew on the one hand,
and John on the other, mention the drink of vinegar
32b Syn. in an entirely different connection). All three synoptics conclude the scene of mockery with the *derision*

Luke S   *by those who are crucified with Jesus,* but here, too, Luke adds special material: only one of the criminals 'rails' at him, the other is outraged by such blasphemy and turns to Jesus, who promises him paradise.

33 Syn.   *Jesus's dying* is introduced in the three synoptic accounts by an almost identical sentence about *dark-*
Luke S   *ness* from the sixth to the ninth hour. But Luke then
Luke ↑   explains the darkness as a solar eclipse and immediately adds the rending of the temple curtain. Only
34ff Matt.   Mark and Matthew mention *the cry of prayer from Ps. 22.1* at the ninth hour, which is misunderstood ('he is calling Elijah') and they then go on to relate the *drink of vinegar* (Ps. 69.21b). Divergences between Mark and Matthew are only matters of style, or are insignificant as far as the content is concerned.

Matt.   Matthew uses the Hebrew 'Eli' instead of the
Mark   Aramaic 'Eloi'; according to Mark the cry was 'at the
Matt.   ninth hour', according to Matthew 'about the ninth
Mark   hour'; Mark has the same bystander speaking, who also brought the sponge with vinegar, whereas
Matt.   according to Matthew 'the others said' that one should wait and see whether Elijah would come.
Luke S   Luke also mentions a cry of prayer 'with a loud voice', but he relates it as *a prayer of trust from Ps. 31.5.* John introduces Jesus's death with the words:
John S   'knowing that all was now finished, (Jesus) said, to
John   fulfil the scripture, "I thirst".' This then leads to the
John S   drink of vinegar and also to what, according to John, are Jesus's last words *'it is finished'.* None of the
37 Ev.   Evangelists narrates the *death of Jesus* with the verb normally used in the New Testament (Jesus 'died'); all use circumlocution: 'Jesus uttered a loud cry and
Mark   breathed his last' (Mark); 'and Jesus cried again with
Matt.   a loud voice and yielded up his spirit' (Matthew);
Luke   'having said this he breathed his last' (Luke); 'and he
John   bowed his head and gave up his spirit' (John).

38 Matt.   *Signs and witnesses* point to the significance of death. Mark only relates a single sign, i.e. the *rending*
(Luke ↑)   *of the temple curtain,* which Luke had already men-
Matt. S.   tioned in connection with the darkness. Matthew adds special material about the *earthquake, splitting rocks, opening tombs, and the appearance of the risen saints* after Jesus has been raised. This is
39 Syn.   followed in all synoptic accounts by the *centurion's confession:*
Mark   'Truly this man was the Son of God' (Mark);
Matt.   'Truly this was the Son of God' (Matthew);

Luke   'Certainly this man was innocent' (or 'righteous') (Luke).

        But there are significant differences in *the intro-*
Mark   *duction to this confession*: according to Mark the centurion 'stood facing him' and confessed, because he 'saw that he thus breathed his last'. According to
Matt.   Matthew not only the centurion, but also 'those who ... with him (kept) watch over Jesus', spoke thus, for they had seen the earthquake and the other occur-
Luke   rences and had been filled with awe. Luke, however, writes that when the centurion saw what had taken place he praised God and made his confession. Only
Luke S   Luke adds that all the *multitudes* who had come to
40ff Syn.   see the sight, returned home beating their breasts. After this Mark and Matthew mention the (accord- ing to Matthew many) *women* who looked on 'from
Luke   afar'. Luke refers more specifically to Ps. 38.11 by writing: 'and all his acquaintances and the women ... stood at a distance ...' In contrast to Mark and Matthew, Luke mentions no names, but like Mark
Mark Matt.   and Matthew he describes them as those who had followed Jesus 'from Galilee' (Matthew, Luke), or 'when he was in Galilee' (Mark) *'followed him'*; Mark and Matthew add further that they had served
Mark S   Jesus. Only Mark mentions *'many other women,*
(John ↑)   who came up with him to Jerusalem'. John mentions the onlooking women earlier. The special material he
John S   now adds also contains meaningful signs: because of Jesus's amazingly rapid death, *his legs are not broken*, and after he is *pierced by a spear, blood and water* flow from his side. Both signs are corroborated by an eyewitness and by the use of a reflective quotation from Scripture are proclaimed as the ful- filment of prophecies.

Bibliography

In each main section, the first reference to a publication gives full details of author, title, place and date of publication. Subsequent references to the same publication give only the name and an abbreviated title.

The Event of the Crucifixion
The Penalty of Crucifixion

General

Blinzler, J., *Der Prozess Jesu.* Regensburg 1969.

Cohn, H., *The Trial and Death of Jesus.* London 1972.

Hitzig, H. F., 'crux' (article in Pauly, A., and Wissowa, G. ed., *Real-Encyklopädie der klassischen Altertumswissenschaft*, NB 1894 ff. IV/2), pp. 1728–1731.

Holzmeister, U., 'Crux Domini eiusque crucifixio ex Archaeologia Romana illustrantur' (*Verbum Domini*, 14, 1934), pp. 149–155, 216–220, 241–249, 257–263.

Peddinghaus, C. D., *Die Entstehung der Leidensgeschichte.* Unpublished thesis, Heidelberg 1965.

The Legal and Political Aspects of Crucifixion

Bammel, E., 'Crucifixion as a Punishment in Palestine' (in Bammel, *The Trial of Jesus*, London 1970), pp. 162–165.

Baumgarten, J. M. 'Does TLH in the Temple Scroll refer to Crucifixion?' (*Journal of Biblical Literature and Exegesis*, 91, 1972), pp. 472–481.

Bovon, F., *Les derniers jours de Jésus.* Neuchâtel 1974.

Brandon, S. G. F., *Jesus and the Zealots: A Study on the Political Factor in Primitive Christianity.* New York 1968.

Cullmann, O., *Jesus und die Revolutionären seiner Zeit.* Tübingen 1970.

Grässer, E., 'Der politisch gekreuzigte Christus: Kritische Anmerkungen zu einer politischen Hermeneutik des

Evangeliums' (in Grässer, *Text und Situation*, Gütersloh 1973), pp. 302–330.

Hengel, M., *Gewalt und Gewaltlosigkeit—Zur 'politischen Theologie' in neutestamentlicher Zeit*. Stuttgart 1971.

Schürer, E., *Geschichte des Jüdischen Volkes im Zeitalter Jesu Christi*. (Leipzig 1901) Hildesheim 1964.

Stauffer, E., *Jerusalem und Rom im Zeitalter Jesu Christi*. Bern 1975.

Weber, H. R., 'Freedom Fighter or Prince of Peace: The current discussion on Jesus and the so-called Zealots' (*Study Encounter*, VIII/4, SE/32, 1972), pp. 1–24 and the literature concerning the subject discussed in that study.

Winter, P., *On the Trial of Jesus*. Berlin 1961.

Archaeological and Medical Findings

Barbet, P., *La Passion du Christ selon le chirurgien*. Paris 1965.

Dr le Bec, 'Le Supplice de la Croix' (*L'Evangile dans la Vie*, April 1925).

Briend, J., 'La Sépulture d'un Crucifié' (*Bible et Terre Sainte*, 133, 1971), pp. 6–10.

Haas, N., 'Anthropological Observations on the Skeletal Remains from Giv'at ha-Mivtar' (*Israel Exploration Journal*, XX, 1970), pp. 38–58.

Hinz, P., *Deus Homo I*. Berlin 1973.

Hynek, R. W., *Le Martyre du Christ*. Avignon 1937. (Original Czech version, 1935).

Ricci, G., *Via crucis secondo la Sindone*, Milan 1972.

Schulte, K. J., 'Der Tod in der Sicht der modernen Medizin' (*Berliner Medizin*, 14, 1963), pp. 177–186, 210–220, Sonderdruck 1–20.

Background Studies in the History of Religion

Bastide, R., 'Les dieux assassinés' (*Lumière et Vie*, XX/101, 1971), pp. 78–88.

Benz, E., 'Der gekreuzigte Gerchte bei Plato, im Neuen Testament und in der alten Kirche' (Abhandlungen der Geistes- und Sozialwissenschaftichen Klasse, 1950/12, Mainz 1950), pp. 1031–1074.

Gusdorf, G., L'Expérience humaine du sacrifice. Paris 1948.

Sources for the Crucifixion of Jesus

Non-Biblical Sources

Classical Authors:
Josephus. *Jewish Antiquities*, 18.3.3.
Tacitus. *Annals*, XV, 44.
Rabbinical Sources:
Klausner, J., *Jesus von Nazareth*. 1952.

New Testamental Apocrypha:

Henneke, E., and Schneemelcher, W., *Neutestamentliche Apokryphen in deutscher Übersetzung* (1958), Vol. 1, pp. 97, 100, 121ff, 163.

Critique of New Testament Sources

Bauer, W., *Rechtgläubigkeit und Ketzerei im ältesten Christentum*. Tübingen 1934, 1964.
Bertram, G., *Die Leidensgeschichte Jesu und der Christuskult: Eine formgeschichtliche Untersuchung*. Göttingen 1922.
Bornkamm, G., *Jesus von Nazareth*. Stuttgart 1960.
Brandon, S. G. F., *Jesus and the Zealots*.
Bultmann, R., *Die Geschichte der synoptischen Tradition*. Göttingen 1961.
— 'Das Verhältnis der urchristlichen Christusbotschaft zum historischen Jesus' (in Bultmann, *Exegetica: Aufsätze zur Erforschung des Neuen Testaments*, Tübingen), pp. 445–469.
Cerfaux, L., *Jésus aux origines de la tradition*. Bruges 1968.
Dibelius, M., *Die Formgeschichte des Evangeliums*. Tübingen 1961.
— 'Zur Formgeschichte der Evangelien' (*Theologische Rundschau*, NF 1, 1929), p. 215.
Dodd, C. H., *The Apostolic Preaching and its Developments*. London 1936.
— *The Founder of Christianity*. London 1970.
Gerhardsson, B., *Memory and Manuscript: Oral Tradition and Written Transmission in Rabbinic Judaism and Early Christianity*. Uppsala 1961.

Hahn, F., 'Die Frage nach dem historischen Jesus und die Eigenart der uns zur Verfügung stehenden Quellen' (In Hahn, F., Lohff, W., Bornkamm, G., *Die Frage nach dem historischen Jesus*, Göttingen 1966), pp. 7–40.

Hanson, R. P. C., 'The Enterprise of Emancipating Christian Belief from History' (in Hanson, A., ed., *Vindications: Essays on the historical basis of Christianity*, London 1966), pp. 29–73.

Klausner, J., *Jesus von Nazareth*.

Köster, H., and Robinson, J. M., *Entwicklungslinien durch die Welt des frühen Christentums*. Tübingen 1971.

Nineham, D. E., 'Some reflections on the present position with regard to the Jesus of history' (in *Historicity and Chronology in the New Testament*, London 1965).

Riesenfeld, H., *The Gospel Tradition and its Beginnings: A Study in the Limits of 'Formgeschichte'*. London 1957.

Schille, G., *Das vorsynoptische Judenchristentum*. Stuttgart 1970.

Trocmé, E., *Jésus de Nazareth vu par les témoins de sa vie*. Neuchâtel 1971.

Historical Problems regarding Christ's Crucifixion

Bartsch, H. W., 'Historische Erwägungen zur Leidensgeschichte' (*Evangelische Theologie* 22, 1962), pp. 449–459.

Blinzler, J., *Prozess*.

Campenhausen, H. von, 'Tod und Auferstehung als "historische Fakten"' (in *Moderne Exegese und historische Wissenschaft:* Dokumentation der Tagung des Deutschen Institutes für Bildung und Wissen, October 1969, Trier 1972), pp. 94–103.

Cohn, H., *Trial*.

Couasnon, Ch., 'Le Golgotha: maquette du sol naturel' (*Bible et Terre Sainte*, 149, 1973), pp. 11–15.

Dodd, C. H., 'The Historical Problem of the Death of Jesus' (in Dodd, *More New Testament Studies*, Manchester 1968), pp. 84–101.

Finegan, J., *The Archaeology of the New Testament*. Princeton 1969.

Jeremias, J., *Die Abendmahlsworte Jesu*. Göttingen 1967.

Parrot, A., *Golgotha et Saint-Sépulcre*. Neuchâtel 1955.

Peddinghaus, C. D., *Leidensgeschichte.*

Sloyan, G. S., *Jesus on Trial:* The development of the Passion Narratives and their Historical and Ecumenical Implications. Philadelphia 1973.

Strobel, A., 'Der Termin des Todes Jesu' (*Zeitschrift für die neutestamentliche Wissenschaft und die Kunde der ältesten Kirche,* LI, 1960), pp. 69–101.

Doubtful Distinction between Event and Interpretation of the Crucifixion

Chambers, M. B., 'Was Jesus Really Obedient unto Death?' (*Journal of Religion,* 50, 1970) pp. 121–138.

Dahl, N. A., 'Der gekreuzigte Messias' (in Ristow and Matthiae, ed., *Der historische Jesus und der kerygmatische Christus,* Berling 1962), pp. 149–169.

Ramsey, I. T., *Religious Language: An Empirical Placing of Theological Phrases.* London 1973.

General Studies regarding Jesus's Crucifixion and its Interpretation in the New Testament

Delling, G., *Der Kreuzestod Jesu in der urchristlichen Verkündigung.* Göttingen 1972.

Kessler, H., *Die theologische Bedeutung des Todes Jesu.* Düsseldorf 1970.

Léon-Dufour, X., 'Passion (Récits de la)' (*Dictionnaire de la Bible,* Supplément XXXV, Paris 1960), pp. 1418–1492.

'La Mort du Christ' (Special number *Lumière et Vie* XX/101, 1971), pp. 34–59.

Schelkle, K. H., *Die Passion Jesu in der Verkündigung des Neuen Testaments.* Heidelberg 1949 (with bibliography for earlier studies of the same sort).

Schrage, W., 'Das Verständnis des Todes Jesu Christi im Neuen Testament' (in Bizer, Goeters, Schrage, Kreck, and Fürst, *Das Kreuz Jesu Christi als Grund des Heils,* Gütersloh 1967), pp. 45–86.

Viering, F., ed. *Zur Bedeutung des Todes Jesu: Exegetische Beiträge.* Gütersloh 1967.

NB: These general studies are presupposed for the following sections and will not be referred to again.

The Earliest Crucifixion Traditions
The 'Bible of the Early Church'

General

Dodd, C. H., *According to the Scriptures:* The sub-structure of New Testament theology. London 1952.

Lindars, B., *New Testament Apologetic:* The Doctrinal Significance of The Old Testament. London 1961.

Sand, A., 'Wie geschrieben steht . . .' Zur Auslegung der jüdischen Schriften in den urchristlichen Gemeinden' (in Ernst, J., ed., *Schriftauslegung:* Beiträge zur Hermeneutik des Neuen Testamentes und im Neuen Testament, Munich, Paderborn, Vienna 1972), pp. 331–357.

Methods of Early Christian Use of Scripture

Betz, O., *Offenbarung und Schriftforschung in der Qumransekte.* Tübingen 1960.

Dahl, N. A., 'Eschatologie und Geschichte im Lichte der Qumrantexte' (*Zeit und Geschichte:* Dankesgabe an R. Bultmann, Tübingen 1964), pp. 3–18.

Lindars, B., *Apologetic.*

Stendahl, K., *The School of Matthew and its Use of the Old Testament.* Philadelphia (1954) 1968.

Old Testament and Interestamental Key Texts for the Interpretation of Jesus's Death

Dibelius, M., *Die Formgeschichte des Evangeliums.* Tübingen 1961.

Dodd, C. H., *Historical Tradition in the Fourth Gospel.* Cambridge 1963.

Flesseman-van Leer, E., 'Die Interpretation der Passionsgeschichte vom Alten Testament aus' (in Viering, ed., *Zur Bedeutung des Todes Jesu:* Exegetische Beiträge, Gütersloh 1967), pp. 79–96.

Lohse, E., 'Die alttestamentlichen Bezüge im neutestamentlichen Zeugnis vom Tode Jesu Christi' (in Viering, ed., *Zur Bedeutung des Todes Jesu:* Exgetische Beiträge, Gütersloh 1967), pp. 97–112.

— *Märtyrer und Gottesknecht:* Untersuchungen zur urchristlichen Verkündigung vom Sühnetod Jesu Christi. Göttingen 1963.

Psalm 22 and the Suffering Righteous

Psalm 22

Dahood, M., *Psalms*, I. New York 1965.

Gélin, A., 'Les quatre lectures du psaume XXII' (*Bible et Vie Chrétienne*, I, 1953), pp. 31–39.

Gese, H., 'Psalm 22 und das Neue Testament: Der älteste Bericht vom Tode Jesu und die Entstehung des Herrenmahles' (*Zeitschrift für Theologie und Kirche*, 65/1, 1968), pp. 1–22.

Fisher, L. E., 'Betrayed by Friends: An expository Study of Psalm 22' (*Interpretation*, 18, 1964), pp. 20–38.

Kraus, H. J., *Psalmen*, I. Neukirchen 1961.

Lange, H. D., 'The Relationship between Psalm 22 and the Passion Narrative' (*Concordia Theological Monthly*, 43/9, 1972), pp. 610–621.

Martin-Achard, R., 'Remarques sur le Psaume 22' (in Martin-Achard, *Approche des Psaumes,* Neuchâtel 1969), pp. 26–40.

Reumann, J. H., 'Psalm 22 at the Cross: Lament and Thanksgiving for Jesus Christ' (*Interpretation*, 28, 1964), pp. 39–58.

Schmid, H. H., '"Mein Gott, mein Gott, warum hast du mich verlassen": Psalm 22 als Beispiel alttestamentlicher Rede von Krankheit und Tod' (*Wort und Dienst*, NF 11, 1971), pp. 119–140.

Westermann, C., *Gewendete Klage:* Eine Auslegung des 22. Psalms. Neukirchen 1957.

The Suffering Righteous

Benz, E., 'Der gekreuzigte Gerechte bei Plato, im Neuen Testamen und in der alten Kirche' (*Abhandlungen der Geistes-und Sozialwissenschaftlichen Klasse*, 1950/12, Mainz 1950), pp. 1031–1074.

Lohse, E., *Märtyrer.*

Ruppert, L., *Der leidende Gerechte:* Eine motivgeschichtliche Untersuchung zum Alten Testament und zwischentestamentlichen Judentum. *Würzburg 1972.*
— *Jesus als der leidende Gerechte?* Der Weg Jesu im Lichte eines alt- und zwischentestamentlichen Motivs. Stuttgart 1972.
Schweizer, E., *Erniedrigung und Erhöhung bei Jesus und seinen Nachfolgern.* Zürich 1962.

The Beginnings of the Passion Narrative(s)

Various Hypotheses

Benoit, P., and Boismard, M. E., *Synopse des Quatre Evangiles,* Tome II, Paris 1972.
Bultmann, R., *Die Geschichte der synoptischen Tradition.* Göttingen 1961.
Dibelius, M., *Formgeschichte.*
— 'Das historische Problem der Leidensgeschichte' (in Dibelius, *Botschaft und Geschichte,* I, Tübingen 1953), pp. 248–257.
Dodd, C. H., *Historical Tradition.*
Finegan, J., *Die Überlieferung der Leidens-und Auferstehungsgeschichte Jesu.* Giessen 1934.
Grant, F. C., *The Earliest Gospel:* Studies of the evangelic tradition at its point of cristallization in writing. New York, Nashville 1943.
Knox, W. L., *The Source of the Synoptic Gospels,* I: St Mark. Cambridge 1953.
Linnemann, E., *Studien zur Passionsgeschichte.* Göttingen 1970.
Peddinghaus, C. D., *Die Entsehung der Leidensgeschichte* (Published thesis). Heidelberg 1965.
Schneider, G., 'Das Problem einer vorkanonischen Passionerzählung' (*Biblische Zeitschrift,* 16, 1972) pp. 222–244.
Schreiber, J., *Theologie des Vertrauens:* Eine redaktionsgeschichtliche Untersuchung des Markusevangeliums. Hamburg 1969.
—*Die Markuspassion:* Wege zur Erforschung der Leidensgeschichte Jesu. Hamburg 1969.

Schweizer, E., *Das Evangelium nach Markus*. Göttingen 1968.

Taylor, V., *The Gospel according to St Mark*. London 1957.

The Origin of the Passion Story and its role in the early Church

Bertram, G., *Die Leidensgeschichte und der Christuskult*. Göttingen 1922.

Dibelius, M., *Formgeschichte*.

Gnilka, J., *Jesus Christus nach frühen Zeugnissen des Glaubens*. Munich 1970.

Pobee, J., 'The cry of the centurion—a cry of defeat' (in Bammel, E., ed., *The Trial of Jesus*, London, 1970), pp. 91–102.

Schille, G., 'Das Leiden des Herrn: Die evangelische Passionstradition und ihr "Sitz im Leben"' (*Zeitschrift für Theologie und Kirche*, 52/2, 1955), pp. 161–205.

—*Das Vorsynoptische Judenchristentum*. Stuttgart 1970.

Crucifixion as Judgement and Turning Point

The Theological Interpretation of the Signs: Darkness, etc.

Bartsch, H. W., 'Die Passions-und Ostergeschichten bei Matthäus' (*Basileia* (Festschrift für W. Freitag), Stuttgart 1959), pp. 27–41.

Benoit and Boismard., *Synopse*, II.

Grayston, K., 'The Darkness of the Cosmic Sea: a Study of Symbolism in Mark's Narrative of the Crucifixion' (*Theology*, LV/382, 1952), pp. 122–127.

Kratz, R., *Auferstehung als Befreiung:* Eine Studie zur Passions- und Auferstehungstheologie bei Matthäus. Stuttgart 1973.

Linnemann, E., *Studien*.

Schreiber, J., *Vertrauen*.

The Rending of the Temple Curtain

de Jonge, M., 'Het voorhangsel in de synoptische Evangelien' and 'Het motief van het gescheurde voorhangsel van de tempel in een aantal vroegchristelijke geschriften' (*Nederlands Theologisch Tijdschrift*, 21, 1967), pp. 90–114, 257–276.

Lindeskok, G., 'The Veil of the Temple' (*Coniectanea Neotestamentica*, XI, Lund 1947), pp. 132–137.

Pelletier, A., 'La Tradition synoptique du "Voile déchiré" à la lumière des réalités archéologiques' (*Recherches de Sciences Religieuses*, XLVI/2, 1958), pp. 161–180.

The Credal Tradition of the early Church

General

Cullmann, O., *Die ersten christlichen Glaubensbekenntnisse.* Zürich 1943.

Deichgräber, R., *Gotteshymnus und Christushymnus in der frühen Christenheit.* Göttingen 1967.

Kramer, W., *Christos Kyrios Gottesohn:* Untersuchungen zu Gebrauch und Bedeutung der christologischen Bezeichnungen bei Paulus und den vorpaulinischen Gemeinden. Zürich and Stuttgart 1963.

Neufeld, V. H., *The Earliest Christian Confessions.* Leiden 1963.

Wengst, K., *Christologische Formeln und Lieder des Urchristentums.* Gütersloh 1972.

The Significance of Isaiah 53 for the Credal Tradition of the early Church

Cullmann, O., *Glaubensbekenntnisse.*

Dodd, C. H., *Scriptures.*

Goppelt, L., 'Geschichtlich wirksames Sterben: Zur Sühnewirkung des Kreuzes' (in *Leben angesichts des Todes*, Thielicke Festschrift, Tübingen 1968), pp. 61–68.

Hahn, F., *Christologische Hoheitstitel:* Ihre Geschichte im frühen Christentum. Göttingen 1963.

Hooker, M. D., *Jesus and the Servant.* London 1959.

Jeremias, J., 'pais theou' (article in *Theologisches Wörterbuch zum Neuen Testament*, V), pp. 676–713.

— 'Zum Problem der Deutung von Jes. 53 im palästinischen Spätjudentum' (in *Aux Sources de la Tradition Chrétienne,* Mélanges M. Goguel, Neuchâtel and Paris 1950), pp. 113–119.

Lohse, E., *Märtyrer.*

Popkes, W., *Christus Traditus:* Eine Untersuchung zum Begriff der Dahingabe im Neuen Testament. Zürich 1967.

Taylor, V., *Jesus and His Sacrifice:* A Study of the Passion Sayings in the Gospels. London 1943.

Wolff, H. W., *Jesaja 53 im Urchristentum.* Berlin 1950.

1 Corinthians 15.3–5

Origin and Structure of the Formula

Conzelmann, H., 'Zur Analyse der Bekenntnisformel 1 Kor 15,3 bis 5' (*Evangelische Theologie,* 25, 1965), pp. 1–11.

Gnilka, J., *Jesus Christus nach frühen Zeugnissen des Glaubens.* Munich 1970.

Hahn, F., *Hoheitstitel.*

Jeremias, J., *Die Abendmahlsworte Jesu.* Göttingen 1967.

Klappert, B., 'Zur Frage des semitischen und griechischen Urtextes von 1 Kor. XV. 3–5' (*New Testament Studies,* 13/2, 1967), pp. 168–173.

Kremer, J., *Das älteste Zeugnis von der Auferstehung Christi:* Eine bibeltheologische Studie zur Aussage und Bedeutung von 1 Kor. 15, 1–11. Stuttgart 1967.

Lehmann, K., *Auferweckt am dritten Tag nach der Schrift.* Freiburg 1969.

Schweizer, E., 'Two New Testament Creeds Compared: 1 Corinthians 15.3–5 and 1 Timothy 3.16' (in Schweizer, *Neotestamentica,* Zürich 1963), pp. 122–135.

Seidensticker, P., 'Das Antiochenische Glaubensbekenntnis 1 Kor. 15.3–7 im Lichte seiner Traditionsgeschichte' (*Theologie und Glaube,* 57, 1967), pp. 286–323.

Wilckens, U., 'Der Ursprung der Überlieferung der Erscheinungen des Auferstandenen: Zur traditionsgeschichtlichen Analyse von 1 Kor. 15.1–11' (in *Dogma und Denkstrukturen,* Festschrift für E. Schlink, Göttingen 1963), pp. 56–95.

The Exegesis of 'Died for our Sins'

See particularly:

van Cangh, M. J., '"Mort pour nos péchés selon les Ecritures" (1 Cor. 15.3b): Une référence à Isaïe 53?' (*Revue Théologique de Louvain*, 1/2, 1970), pp. 191–199.

Dahl, N. A., 'Der gekreuzigte Messias' (in Ristow, H., and Matthiae, K., ed., *Der historische Jesus und der kerygmatische Christus*, Berlin 1961), pp. 159ff.

Gnilka, J., *Jesus Christus*.

Hahn, F., *Hoheitstitel*.

Lehmann, K., *Auferweckt am dritten Tag*.

Riesenfeld, H., 'hyper' (*Theologisches Wörterbuch zum Neuen Testament*, VIII), pp. 510–518.

Seidensticker, P., *Das Antiochenische Glaubensbekenntnis*.

Pauline Interpretations of the Cross

Paul, the Apostle of Christ

Paul's Cultural Environment

Davies, W. D., *Paul and Rabbinic Judaism:* some rabbinic elements in Pauline theology. London 1948.

Hugede, N., *Saint Paul et la Culture Grecque*. Geneva 1966.

Wendland, P., *Die hellenistisch-römische Kultur in ihren Beziehungen zum Judentum und Christentum*. Tübingen 1972.

Paul and the Old Testament

Ellis, E. E., *Paul's Use of the Old Testament*. Edinburgh and London 1957.

Käsemann, E., 'Geist und Buchstabe' (in Kaesemann, *Paulinische Perspektiven*, Tübingen 1969), pp. 237–285.

Lindars, B., *New Testament Apologetic:* The Doctrinal Significance of the Old Testament. London 1961.

Vielhauer, P., 'Paulus und das Alte Testament' (in *Studien zur Geschichte und Theologie der Reformation*, Festschrift E. Bizer, Neukirchen 1969), pp. 33–62.

The Pauline Concept of Faith

Cerfaus, L., *Christus in der Paulinischen Theologie*. Düsseldorf 1964. (Original French edition, Paris 1951).

Eichholz, G., *Die Theologie des Paulus im Umriss*. Neukirchen 1972.

Kaesemann, E., *Paulinische Perspektiven*.

Paul the Missionary

Bornkamm, G., 'Das missionarische Verhalten des Paulus nach 1 Kor. 9.19–23 und in der Apostelgeschichte' (in Bornkamm, *Geschichte und Glaube*, II, Munich 1971), pp. 149–161.

Hass, O., *Paulus der Missionar*. Münsterschwarzach 1971.

Pauline Theology of the Cross

Chevallier, M.-A., 'La prédictation de la croix' (*Etudes Théologiques et Religieuses*, 45, 1970), pp. 131–161.

Luz, U., 'Theologia crucis als Mitte der Theologie im Neuen Testament' (*Evangelische Theologie*, 34, 1974), pp. 116–141.

Ortkemper, F. J., *Das Kreuz in der Verkündigung des Apostels Paulus*. Stuttgart 1967.

Wiencke, G., *Paulus über Jesu Tod:* Die Deutungen des Todes Jesu bei Paulus und ihre Herkunft. Gütersloh 1939.

1 Corinthians 1.18ff

Commentaries

Conzelmann, H., *Der erste Brief an die Korinther*. Göttingen 1969.

Lietzmann, H. and Kümmel, W. G., *An die Korinther I/II*. Tübingen 1949.

The Cultural Situation at Corinth

Conzelmann, H., 'Korinth und die Mädchen der Aphrodite: zur Religionsgeschichte der Stadt Korinth' (in Conzelmann, *Theologie als Schriftauslegung:* Aufsätze zum Neuen Testament, Munich 1974) pp. 152–166.

Lengschau, T., 'Korinthos' (article in Pauly, A., and Wissowa, G., *Real-Encyklopädie der klassischen Altertumswissenschaft*, Suppl. IV, 1924), pp. 991–1036.

de Waele, F. J., 'Korinthos' (article in Pauly, A., and Wis-

BIBLIOGRAPHY

sowa, G., *Real-Encyklopädie der klassischen Altertums-wissenschaft*, Suppl. VI, 1935), pp. 182–200.

The Religious Situation of the Corinthians

Conzelmann, H., *Der erste Brief.*

Fascher, E., 'Die Korintherbriefe und die Gnosis' (in Tröger, K. W., ed., *Gnosis und Neues Testament*, Gütersloh 1973), pp. 281–291.

Luetgert, W., *Freiheitspredigt und Schwarmgeister in Korinth:* Ein Beitrag zur Charakteristik der Christuspartei. Gütersloh 1908.

Martyn, J. L., 'Epistemology at the turn of the Ages: 2 Corinthians 5.16' (in *Christian History and Interpretation*, Studies presented to John Knox, Cambridge 1967), pp. 269–287.

Munck, J., 'Die Gemeinde ohne Parteien: Studien über 1 Kor. 1–4' (in Munck, *Paulus und die Heilsgeschichte*, Aarhus and Copenhagen 1954), pp. 127–161.

Schlatter, A., *Die korinthische Theologie.* Gütersloh 1914.

Schmithals, W., *Die Gnosis in Korinth:* Eine Untersuchung zu den Korintherbriefen. Göttingen 1965 (first published 1956).

Wilckens, U., *Weisheit und Torheit:* eine exegetisch-religionsgeschichtliche Untersuchung zu 1 Kor. 1 und 2. Tübingen 1959.

The Reason for Writing 1 Corinthians

Besides the above mentioned literature, see especially:

Dahl, N. A., 'Paul and the Church at Corinth in 1 Cor. 1.10–4.21' (in *Christian History and Interpretation*, Studies presented to John Knox, Cambridge 1967), pp. 313–335.

Old Testament and Intertestamental Reflection on Scripture in Connection with 1 Corinthians 1.18ff

Cerfaux, L., 'Vestiges d'un florilège dans 1 Cor. 1.18–3.24?' (*Revue d'Histoire Ecclésiastique*, XXVII/I, 1931), pp. 521–534.

Ellis, E. E., *Paul's Use.*

Munck, J., *Gemeinde.*

Peterson, E., '1 Kor 1.18ff und die Thematik des jüdischen Busstages' (*Biblica*, 32, 1951), pp. 97–103.

Wilckens, U., *Weisheit*.

The Exegesis of 1 Corinthians 1.18ff

Particulary:

Conzelmann, H., *Der erste Brief.*

Eichholz, G., *Theologie.*

Luz, U., *Theologia crucis.*

Müller, K., '1 Kor. 1.18—25. *Die eschatologisch-kritische Funktion der Verkündigung des Kreuzes*' (*Biblische Zeitschrift*, 10, 1966), pp. 246–272.

Ortkemper, F. J., *Kreuz.*

Galatians 3.13ff

Commentaries

Bonnard, P., *L'Epître de Saint Paul aux Galates.* Neuchâtel 1972.

Mussner, F., *Der Galaterbrief.* Freiburg/Basel/Wien 1974.

Oepke, A., *Der Brief des Paulus an die Galater.* Berlin 1957.

Schlier, H., *Der Brief an die Galater.* Göttingen 1962.

The Religious and Cultural Situation of the Galatians

Betz, H. D., 'Geist, Freiheit und Gesetz: Die Botschaft des Paulus an die Gemeinden in Galatien' (*Zeitschrift für Theologie und Kirche*, 71, 1974), pp. 78–93.

Brandis, 'Galatia, Galatiké (chora), Gallograikia' (article in Pauly, A., and Wissowa, G., *Real-Encyklopädie der klassischen Altertumswissenschaft*, XIII), pp. 519–559.

Stähelin, F., *Geschichte der kleinasiatischen Galater.* Leipzig 1907.

Steinmann, A., *Der Leserkreis des Galaterbriefes.* Münster 1908.

de Vries, J., *Keltische Religion.* Stuttgart 1961.

The Reason for Writing Galatians, and Paul's Adversaries

Betz, H. D., *Geist.*

Borse, U., *Der Standort des Galaterbriefes.* Cologne 1972.

Eckert, J., *Die urchristliche Verkündigung im Streit zwischen*

Paulus und seinen Gegnern nach dem Galaterbrief. Munich 1971.

Jewett, R., 'The Agitators and the Galatian Congregation' (*New Testament Studies*, 17, 1971), pp. 198–212.

Mussner, F., *Galaterbrief.*

Schmithals, W., 'Die Häretiker in Galatien' (*Zeitschrift für die neutestamentliche Wissenschaft und die Kunde der älteren Kirche*, 47, 1956), pp. 25–67.

Old Testament and Intertestamental Reflection on Scripture in Connection with Galatians 3.13ff

Dietzfelbinger, Ch., *Paulus und das Alte Testament:* Die Hermeneutik des Paulus, untersucht an seiner Deutung der Gestalt Abrahams. Munich 1961.

Köster, H., 'Gnomai Diaphoroi: Ursprung und Wesen der Mannigfaltigkeit in der Geschichte des frühen Christentums' (in Köster/Robinson *Entwicklungslinien durch die Welt des frühen Christentums*) Tübingen 1971.

Lindars, B., *Apologetic.*

Mussner, F., *Galaterbrief.*

The Exegesis of Galatians 3.13ff

Particularly:

Betz, H. D., *Geist.*

Hooker, M. D., 'Interchange in Christ' (*The Journal of Theological Studies*, XXII/2, 1971), pp. 349–361.

Kaesemann, E., *Paulinische Perspektiven.*

Lyonnet, S., 'L'Emploi paulinien de "exagorazein" au sens de "redimere" est-il attesté dans la littérature grecque?' (*Biblica*, 42, 1962), pp. 85–89.

Pax, E., 'Der Loskauf: Zur Geschichte eines neutestamentlichen Begriffes' (*Antonianum*, 37, 1962), pp. 239–278.

Wilckens, U., 'Was heisst bei Paulus: "Aus Werken des Gesetzes wird niemand gerecht"?' (*Evangelisch-katholischer Kommentar zum Neuen Testament*, Vorarbeiten Heft I, Zürich and Neukriche 1969), pp. 51–77.

The Crucifixion in the Gospels
General Studies on the Passion Narratives in the Gospels

Bartsch, H. W., 'Die Bedeutung des Sterbens Jesu nach den Synoptikern' (*Theologische Zeitschrift*, 20, 1964), pp. 87–102.

Benoit, P., *Passion et Résurrection du Seigneur*. Paris 1966.

Conzelmann, H., 'Historie und Theologie in den synoptischen Passionsberichten' (in Viering, F., ed., *Zur Bedeutung des Todes Jesu*) Gütersloh 1968.

Martinez, E. R., *The Gospel Accounts of the Death of Jesus: a Study of the Death Accounts made in the Light of the New Testament Traditions, the Redaction and the Theology of the Four Evangelists*. Rome 1970.

Schneider, G., *Die Passion Jesu nach den drei älteren Evangelien*. Munich 1973.

Vanhoye, A., 'Structure et théologie des récits de la Passion dans les évangiles synoptiques' (*Nouvelle Revue Théologique*, 99, 1967), pp. 135–163.

Synopses

Aland, K., ed., *Synopsis Quattuor Evangeliorum*. Stuttgart 1964.

Benoit, P., and Boismard, M. E., *Synopse des Quatre Evangiles*. Tome I. Paris 1965.

Morgenthaler, R., *Statistische Synopse*. Zürich and Stuttgart 1971.

Schmid, J., *Synopse der drei ersten Evangelien* (mit Beifügung der Johannes Parallelen). Regensburg 1968.

The Literary Interdependence of the Gospels

Benoit, P., and Boismard, M. E., *Synopse des Quartre Evangiles*. Tome II. Paris 1972.

Dahl, N. A., 'Die Passionsgeschichte bei Matthäus' (*New Testament Studies*, 2, 1955), pp. 15–32.

Dauer, A., *Die Passionsgeschichte im Johannesevangelium: Eine traditionsgeschichtliche und theologische Untersuchung zu Joh. 18.1–19.30*. Munich 1972.

Léon-Dufour, X., '(Mt et Mc dans le récit de la Passion' (*Biblica*, 40, 1959), pp. 684–696.
Taylor, V., *The Passion Narrative of St Luke*. Cambridge 1972.

The Gospel of the Crucifixion According to Mark

The Gospel of Mark and the Situation of its Readers

Delorme, J., 'Aspects doctrinaux du Second Evangile: études récentes de la rédaction de Marc' (in de la Potterie, I., ed., *De Jésus aux Evangiles:* Tradition et Rédaction dans les Evangiles synoptiques. Gembloux and Paris 1967), pp. 74–99.
Nineham, D. E., *Saint Mark*. Pelican Commentaries 1963.
Rhode, J., *Die redaktionsgeschichtliche Methode.* Hamburg 1966.
Robinson, J. M., *Das Geschichtsverständnis des Markus-Evangeliums.* Zürich 1956.
Schreiber, J., *Theologie des Vertrauens:* Eine redaktionsgeschichtliche Untersuchung des Markusevangeliums. Hamburg 1967.
Schweizer, E., *Das Evangelium nach Markus.* Göttingen 1968.
— 'Anmerkungen zur Theologie des Markus' (in Schweizer, *Neotestamentica*, Zürich and Stuttgart 1963), pp. 93–104.
— 'Die theologische Leistung des Markus' (in Schweizer, *Beiträge zur Theologie des Neuen Testamentes*, Neutestamentliche Aufsätze, 1955–1970. Zurich 1970), pp. 21–42.
Vielhauer, Ph., 'Erwägungen zur Christologie des Markusevangeliums' (in Dinkler, E., ed., *Zeit und Geschichte*, Bultmann Festschrift, Tübingen 1964), pp. 155–169.

Marcan Reflection about the Passion

Maurer, C., 'Knecht Gottes and Sohn Gottes im Passionsbericht des Markusevangeliums' (*Zeitschrift für Theologie und Kirche*, 50, 1953), pp. 1–38.
Sand, A., '"Wie geschrieben steht . . ." Zur Auslegung der jüdischen Schriften in den urchristlichen Gemeinden' (in

Ernst, J., ed., *Schriftauslegung*, Munich, Paderborn, and Vienna 1972), pp. 331–357.

Suhl, A., *Die Funktion der alttestamentlichen Zitate und Anspielungen im Markusevangelium*. Gütersloh 1965.

Marcan Redaction of the Crucifixion

Besides the studies mentioned above, see:

Best., E., *The Temptation and the Passion:* the Marcan Soteriology. Cambridge 1965.

Chevallier, M.-A., 'La prédication de la croix' (*Etudes Théologiques et Religieuses*, 45, 1970), pp. 131–161.

Danker, F. W., 'The Demonic Secret in Mark: A Re-examination of the Cry of Dereliction (15.34)' (*Zeitschrift für neutestamentliche Wissenschaft und die Kunde der älteren Kirche*, 61, 1970), pp. 48–69.

Kiddle, M., 'The Death of Jesus and the Admission of the Gentiles in St Mark' (*The Journal of Theological Studies*, 35, 1934), pp. 45–50.

Luz, U., 'Theologia crucis als Mitte der Theologie im Neuen Testament' (*Evangelische Theologie*, 34, 1974), pp. 116–141.

Peddinghaus, C. D., *Die Entstehung der Leidensgeschichte* (Dissertation). Heidelberg 1965.

Plastaras, J., 'Transfiguration and Cross in the Gospel according to Mark' (*Vincentian Studies*, New York 1968), pp. 13–29.

Schenk, W., 'Die gnostisierende Deutung des Todes Jesu und ihre kritische Interpretation durch den Evangelisten Markus' (in Tröger, K. W., ed., *Gnosis und Neues Testament*, Gütersloh 1973), pp. 231–243.

Trilling, W., 'Der Tod Jesu, Ende der alten Weltzeit (Mk 15.33–41)' (in Trilling, *Christusverkündigung in den synoptischen Evangelien*, Munich 1969), pp. 191–211.

The Gospel of the Crucifixion according to Matthew

The Gospel of Matthew and the Situation of its Readers

Albright, W. F., and Mann, C. S., *Matthew*. New York 1971.

Bonnard, P., *L'Evangile selon Saint Matthieu*. Neuchâtel 1963, 1970.

Bornkamm, G., Barth, G., and Held, H. J., *Überlieferung und Auslegung im Matthäus-Evangelium*. Neunkirchen 1968.

Grundmann, W., *Das Evangelium nach Matthäus*. Berlin 1968, 1971.

Hummerl, R., *Die Auseinandersetzung zwischen Kirche und Judentum im Matthäusevangelium*. Munich 1966.

Rademakers, J., *Au fil de l'évangile selon saint Matthieu*. Heverlee and Louvain 1972.

Schweizer, E., *Das Evangelium nach Matthäus*. Göttingen 1973.

— 'Gesetz und Enthusiasmus bei Matthäus' (in Schweizer, *Beiträge zur Theologie des Neuen Testamentes*), pp. 47–70.

Strecker, G., *Der Weg zur Gerechtigkeit:* Untersuchung zur Theologie des Matthäus. Göttingen 1962.

Suggs, M. J., *Wisdom, Christology and Law in Matthew's Gospel*. Cambridge 1970.

van Tilborg, S., *The Jewish Leaders in Matthew*. Leiden 1972.

Trilling, W., *Das wahre Israel:* Studien zur Theologie des Matthäus-Evangeliums. Munich 1964.

Walker, R., *Die Heilsgeschichte im ersten Evangelium*. Göttingen 1967.

Matthean Reflection about the Passion

Gundry, R. H., *The Use of the Old Testament in St Matthew's Gospel:* with special reference to the messianic hope. Leiden 1967.

Lindars, B., *New Testament Apologetic:* The Doctrinal Significance of the Old Testament. London 1961.

McConnell, R. S., *Law and Prophecy in Matthew's Gospel:* The Authority and Use of the Old Testament in the Gospel of St Matthew. Basle 1969.

Rothfuchs, W., *Die Erfüllungszitate des Matthäusevangeliums*. Stuttgart 1969.

Sand, A., *Wie geschrieben steht.*

Stendahl, K., *The School of Matthew and its Use of the Old Testament*. Philadelphia 1968.

The Matthean Redaction of the Crucifixion

Besides the studies mentioned above see:

Bartsch, H. W., 'Die Passions- und Ostergeschichten bei Matthäus' (*Basileia*, Festschrift for W. Freitag, Stuttgart 1959), pp. 27–41.

Dahl, N. A., *Passionsgeschichte*.

Fischer, K. M., 'Redaktionsgeschichtliche Bemerkungen zur Passionsgeschichte des Matthäus' (in Rogge, J., and Schille, G., ed, *Theologische Versuche*, II, Berlin 1970), pp. 109–128.

Gerhardson, B., 'Jésus livré et abandonné d'après la Passion selon Saint Matthieu' (*Revue Biblique*, 76, 1969), pp. 206–227.

Kratz, R., *Auferweckung als Befreiung:* Eine Studie zur Passions- und Auferstehungstheologie des Matthäus. Stuttgart 1973.

van Stempvoot, P. A., ' "Goods Zoon" of "En Zoon Gods" in Matth 27.54?' (*Nederlands Theologisch Tijdschrift* 9, 1954), pp. 79–89.

The Gospel of the Crucifixion according to Luke

The Gospel of Luke and the Situation of its Readers

Caird, B. C., *Saint Luke*. Pelican N.T. Commentaries 1963.

Conzelmann, H., *Die Mitte der Zeit:* Studien zur Theologie des Lukas. Tübingen 1964.

Ellis, E. E., *The Gospel of Luke*. London 1966.

Grundmann, W., *Das Evangelium nach Lukas*. Berlin 1961.

Lohfink, G., *Die Himmelfahrt Jesu:* Untersuchungen zu den Himmelfahrts- und Erhöhungstexten bei Lukas. Munich 1971.

Minear, P., 'Dear Theo: the kerygmatic intention and claim of the Book of Acts' (*Interpretation*, XXVII, 1973), pp. 131–150.

Rhode, J., *Redaktionsgeschichtliche Methode*.

Thompson, G. H. P., *The Gospel according to Luke*. Oxford 1972.

Wilckens, U., *Die Missionsreden der Apostelgeschichte.* Neukirchen 1963.

Lucan Scriptural Meditation about the Passion

Dibelius, M., *Die Formgeschichte des Evangeliums.* Tübingen 1961.

Rese, M., *Alttestamentliche Motive in der Christologie des Lukas.* Gütersloh 1969.

The Lucan Redaction of the Crucifixion

Besides the studies mentioned above see:

George, A., 'Le sens de la mort de Jésus pour Luc' (*Revue Biblique*, 80, 1973), pp. 186–217.

Grelot, P., 'Aujourd'hui tu seras avec moi dans le Paradis (Luc XXIII.43) (*Revue Biblique*, 74, 1967), pp. 194–214.

Kiddle, M., 'The Passion Narrative in St Luke's Gospel' (*The Journal of Theological Studies*, 36, 1935), pp. 267–280.

Kilpatrick, G. D., 'A Theme of the Lucan Passion Story and Luke XXIII.47' (*The Journal of Theological Studies*, 43, 1942), pp. 34–36.

Lohse, E., *Märtyrer und Gottesknecht:* Untersuchung zur urchristlichen Verkündigung vom Sühnetod Jesu Christi. Göttingen 1963.

Schütz, F., *Der leidende Christus:* die angefochtene Gemeinde und das Christuskerygma. Stuttgart, Berlin, Cologne, Mainz 1969.

Stalder, K., 'Die Heilsbedeutung des Todes Jesu in den lukanischen Schriften' (*Internationale Kirchliche Zeitschrift*, 52, 1962), pp. 222–242.

Zehnle, R., 'The salvific character of Jesus' death in Lucan soteriology' (*Theological Studies*, 30, 1969), pp. 420–444.

The Gospel of the Crucifixion according to John

The Gospel of John and the Situation of its Readers

Besides older commentaries by C. K. Barrett (1955), E. C. Hoskyns (1947), M. J. Lagrange (1925), R. H. Lightfoot (1956), see:

Brown, R. E., *The Gospel according to John*, New York I 1966, II 1970.

Bultmann, R., *Das Evangelium des Johannes*. Göttingen 1941, 1969.

Schulz, S., *Das Evangelium nach Johannes*. Göttingen 1971.

Vouga, F., '"Aimez-vous les uns les autres": Une étude sur l'Eglise de Jean' (*Bulletin du Centre Protestant d'Etudes*, 26/3, 1974), pp. 5–31.

John's Reflection on Scripture

Barrett, C. K., 'The Old Testament in the Fourth Gospel' (*The Journal of Theological Studies*, XLVII, 1947), pp. 155–169.

Dauer, A., *Passionsgeschichte*.

Dibelius, M., 'Die alttestamentlichen Motive in der Leidensgeschichte des Petrus- und Johannesevangeliums' (in Dibelius, *Botschaft und Geschichte*, I) Tübingen 1953).

Dodd, C. H., *Historical Tradition in the Fourth Gospel*. Cambridge 1963.

Freed, E. D., *Old Testament Quotations in the Gospel of John*. Leiden 1965.

John's Redaction of the Crucifixion

Besides the commentaries mentioned above see:

Dauer, A., *Passionsgeschichte* (with extensive bibliography).

Haenchen, E., 'Historie und Geschichte in den johanneischen Passionsberichten' (in Viering, F., ed., *Zur Bedeutung des Todes Jesu*, Gütersloh 1968), pp. 55–78.

Kaesemann, E., *Jesu letzter Wille nach Johannes 17*. Tübingen 1967.

Riaud, J., 'La Gloire et la Royauté de Jésus dans la passion selon Saint Jean' (*Bible et Vie Chrétienne*, 56, 1964), pp. 28–44.

Thüsing, W., *Die Erhöhung und Verherrlichung Jesu im Johannesevangelium*. Münster 1970.

Vergote, A., 'L'Exaltation du Christ en croix selon le quatrième Evangile' (*Ephemerides Theologicae Lovanienses*, 1952), pp. 5–23.